T0219947

Oracle Incident Response and Forensics

Preparing for and Responding to Data Breaches

Pete Finnigan

Apress®

Oracle Incident Response and Forensics

Pete Finnigan
Acomb York, North Yorkshire, United Kingdom

ISBN-13 (pbk): 978-1-4842-3263-7   ISBN-13 (electronic): 978-1-4842-3264-4
https://doi.org/10.1007/978-1-4842-3264-4

Library of Congress Control Number: 2017961732

Copyright © 2018 by Pete Finnigan

Cover image designed by Freepik

Managing Director: Welmoed Spahr
Editorial Director: Todd Green
Acquisitions Editor: Jonathan Gennick
Development Editor: Laura Berendson
Coordinating Editor: Jill Balzano
Copy Editor: Kezia Endsley
Compositor: SPi Global
Indexer: SPi Global
Artist: SPi Global

Distributed to the book trade worldwide by Springer Science+Business Media New York, 233 Spring Street, 6th Floor, New York, NY 10013. Phone 1-800-SPRINGER, fax (201) 348-4505, e-mail orders-ny@springer-sbm.com, or visit www.springeronline.com. Apress Media, LLC is a California LLC and the sole member (owner) is Springer Science + Business Media Finance Inc (SSBM Finance Inc). SSBM Finance Inc is a **Delaware** corporation.

For information on translations, please e-mail rights@apress.com, or visit http://www.apress.com/rights-permissions.

Apress titles may be purchased in bulk for academic, corporate, or promotional use. eBook versions and licenses are also available for most titles. For more information, reference our Print and eBook Bulk Sales web page at http://www.apress.com/bulk-sales.

Any source code or other supplementary material referenced by the author in this book is available to readers on GitHub via the book's product page, located at www.apress.com/9781484232637. For more detailed information, please visit http://www.apress.com/source-code.

Printed on acid-free paper

Table of Contents

TABLE OF CONTENTS

About the Author

Pete Finnigan is the founder and CEO of PeteFinnigan.com Limited, a company based in York, UK that specializes in helping customers secure data held in their Oracle databases. He has assisted customers all over the world in performing security audits of their Oracle databases, Oracle incident response and forensics, design and implementation work on Oracle features such as Virtual Private Database (VPD), encryption, masking, and many more services. Finnigan also provides very popular detailed training around many aspects of Oracle security. Pete has spoken many times at conferences around the world on the subject of Oracle security.

Pete Finnigan is an Oracle ACE for security and also a member of The OAKTable, which is a network of Oracle scientists. Pete graduated from the University in Leeds, UK in 1995 with a first-class honors degree in electronics and electrical systems. This was achieved on a part-time basis while working a full-time job.

Pete is also the author of the book *SANS Oracle Step-by Step Guide* versions 1 and 2 and a co-author on the book *Expert Oracle Practices*. He can be found on LinkedIn, Facebook, Twitter, and his company's web site at http://www.petefinnigan.com

Acknowledgments

First of all I would like to thank my beautiful wife, Zulia, for her support while I wrote this book. I would also like to thank my children, Emil and Eric, for supporting my Oracle security endeavors.

I would also like to thank Jonathan Gennick for approaching me to write this book. Jonathan is very professional and a really nice person to boot.

Introduction

Data breaches are now so commonplace that it has become a matter for national news channels and unskilled discussions. Even the BBC no longer brings in a security expert to discuss the latest data loss; it is just reported as a matter of fact. A bank robber of old with a sawed-off shotgun stealing sacks of money is now a hacker for hire with USBs and discs of data for sale to fuel identity theft, spamming, card theft, and much more. Companies now have to assume that if they process personal, finance, or indeed any valuable data and hold that data in an Oracle database then they are targets.

Regulatory bodies and governments are now taking data breaches much more seriously. For instance, here in the UK a body was formed in recent years called the information Commissioner's office specifically to deal with protection of privacy and data for the public. In the United States, regulations such as Sarbanes Oxley (SOX), Gramm Leach Bliley (GLBA), and the Health Insurance Portability and Accountability (HIPPA) were also created to regulate data and to protect privacy. Most American states and indeed a lot of other countries now follow California with its data breach notification law—California S.B. 1386—in having implemented similar laws.

In Europe each of the 28 member states of the EU will soon, at the start of 2018, implement a new data protection act called GDPR. This new EU law will affect not just EU but any country that processes and stores the personal data of EU citizens. This law will be far-reaching and will include the right for citizens' data to be forgotten, the need to know where you have stored customers' personal data, the need to know that there was a breach, and the need to notify.

These are just a small number of examples of some data protection laws, and most countries have similar laws. The upshot is you must be able to respond to a data breach, to understand what happened and how, to understand which data was breached, to report the breach, and know how to secure your systems to prevent a similar breach from happening again.

This creates the need for two new skills that the Oracle practitioner should acquire or hone:

- **Incident response:** This is the process and rules that you should follow if there is a breach of your Oracle database. Each and any data breach may be different in content and character, so understanding what a breach looks like and whether it really is a breach is important. An incident response process or policy will also include details of the actions to be performed, the people (or job roles in your organization) and tools to be used, and the types of data and evidence to be collected.

- **Forensic analysis:** This involves the steps taken to analyze the data collected and the techniques and tools that can be used to locate evidence of an attacker and ideally also when, where, how, and by whom the attack was conducted. As the CSI show made famous on television, the forensic process is about analyzing and detecting detailed facts and snippets of information to answer these questions.

Incident response and forensics are inextricably linked; carrying out an incident response isn't valuable unless a forensic analysis of the collected data (artifacts) is also performed. Conversely, simply carrying out forensic analysis of "something" does not carry weight unless it's part of a complete process.

With each day that passes, more and more data breaches are occurring; as I write this, it has just been reported that Equifax had been breached and 143 million customer account details were taken. Cex, the large second-hand retailer, lost 2 million account details and Verizon lost six million. See `http://www.wired.co.uk/article/hacks-data-breaches-2017` for more information.

About This Book

As an Oracle DBA, developer, or security person, how do you know that your Oracle database has been breached and, more importantly, what do you do about it? How do you investigate a complex and often huge system to understand if the breach is real and to then know what was taken or seen by the hacker? How did the attackers get in; what did they see; what could they have done, and how much further could they have gone with more skill? Often companies are lucky that the attackers do not know Oracle and simply use free web based tools to attack a database. If they really knew Oracle, then the results could have been much worse.

This book describes what a breach or incident is and discusses what steps and processes should be taken if a breach is suspected. The book also looks at what forensics is in relation to Oracle and what tools and techniques are available, as well as which should be used to investigate a database to find out how the breach occurred, who did it, and why. The book also discusses how to put everything together to create a holistic approach to the investigation. Finally, the book looks briefly at what should now be put in place in "your" databases to make an attack harder but also to aid detection of a future attack and make any incident response and investigation easier.

There has been very little written about Oracle forensics and incident response over the years since I was the first to write about Oracle forensics when I wrote a module for the original SANS Oracle Security 509 class back in 2004. I have written a number of papers and presentations, as has David Litchfield, but in comparison to the subject of Oracle security in general not much exists on Oracle forensics and even less exists on incident response. This book fills this gap and allows Oracle professionals to get a grasp of Oracle forensics and incident response.

Who Should Read This Book

The focus of this book is the response to an Oracle database data breach and the subsequent forensics analysis of the database. The book is aimed at the Oracle professional—the DBA, developer, and managers of Oracle teams and in general anyone who is concerned with storing data in an Oracle database. The key messages of the book transcend both the work of the DBA and security professionals. In general, security professionals are not going to be experts at Oracle so they need to involve the DBA in a potential forensic analysis. Developers will benefit from understanding how the tracks of an attacker can be traced to an Oracle database and therefore prepare their applications that fit in the database to potentially include additional sources of tracking information. The security professional will get a grasp of how forensic information can be extracted from an Oracle database.

How This Book Is Organized

This book starts off with the basics by covering what a breach is, what an incident is, and what Oracle forensics and Oracle incident responses are. It then looks at how a security professional or a DBA can extract forensic data from an Oracle database and from where in the Oracle database. The book then goes on to discuss incident response processes, reacting to incidents, and of course forensic analysis, including some examples.

The book finishes with an overview of what to do next to help ensure that you are ready for any potential Oracle breach incident and ready and able to forensically analyze your database. The chapters of the book cover the following issues and features.

- **Chapter 1—Data Breach:** The book starts by defining what a data breach is, what an incident is, and how breaches occur. Then Oracle forensics and forensics in general are introduced. The chapter ends with a brief look at how Oracle works at a high level, as this is the basis for finding forensic telltales in the database to determine what an attacker did.

- **Chapter 2—Artifacts:** Telltale signs of actions conducted in the database can be determined; these can be database specific or outside of the database. Consideration is given to many of the possible places in the database and outside of the database from where evidence can be extracted. This chapter also considers accountability and identity traces in the database as well as the problem of time. One of the key tenants of forensic analysis is to establish all of the evidence in a time-based format. This chapter finishes with a discussion of the problem of tracking read access as well as ways to establish if data or objects have been deleted.

- **Chapter 3—Incident Response Approach:** This section of the book is the most important, as it considers how to plan for an incident and create an incident response approach and policy. We also explore the role of the incident coordinator and the need to create a team to react to a breach. A very important part of an incident response is to have a set of tools ready and able to collect evidence from the database.

- **Chapter 4—Reacting to an Incident:** Before any response to an incident starts, it is very important to establish the things you should not do. So these are covered first. The chapter discusses the steps that should be followed, including ad hoc and scripted collection of artifacts. Also discussed is the issue of disconnecting the database from the network, shutting it down, and potentially restoring, rebuilding, or correcting it.

- **Chapter 5—Forensic Analysis:** This chapter focuses on the analysis of a potential hack in an example system. This example brings together a lot of the techniques discussed so far in the book. Pre-analysis steps as well as post-analysis steps are considered along with findings and assumptions and creating a report and summary.

- **Chapter 6—What To Do Next:** We close the book with a summary whose focus is to give some ideas of what you should do now, before you are actually breached. This clearly includes taking steps to secure the Oracle database to prevent a breach in the first place and enabling sophisticated audit trails to ease the process of incident response and forensic analysis.

Scripts and Download

Much of the SQL code that is presented in the book is available as scripts from the author's web site. The example code can be downloaded from `http://www.petefinnigan.com/forensics/download.zip`.

CHAPTER 1

Data Breach

There are often multiple reasons why an Oracle database may be attacked. An attacker may see an Oracle database simply as an easy target to gain access to a company's other IT infrastructure. Unfortunately, because Oracle is a very complex product that requires an enormous amount of configuration, often gaps are created in the security model used to protect the data held within the database.

Because access to data is often at multiple levels—via an application interface, a developer using TOAD, a DBA using SQL*Plus, and many more—there is a risk that the security controls are different at each layer and so allow access to more data at one layer than another. An attacker may choose to attack an Oracle database to steal the data or he may choose to attack an Oracle database simply to gain access to other IT infrastructure.

It is important to understand at a high level the types of attacks that can be performed on an Oracle database so that you are able to recognize them from evidence gathered. It is also imperative to understand what an incident is and what an incident response is. Following an incident, forensic analysis must take place to understand how the attackers may have breached and stolen data or done other damage to your database. Finally, it's important to know how Oracle itself works at a reasonably detailed level because this will give you clues as to where evidence or artifacts can be found and used.

© Pete Finnigan 2018
P. Finnigan, *Oracle Incident Response and Forensics*,
https://doi.org/10.1007/978-1-4842-3264-4_1

We have a brief discussion of the subject of chain of custody. This is the process normally used when investigating a PC as part of computer forensics. With a small system, the process is often clean and simple and involves documentation, verification, and secure storage of the artifacts (usually a complete computer or hard disk). A short discussion is also included on the issue of admissibility of evidence in court. Verifying evidence is usually done by checksumming hard disk, and this process is compared with an Oracle database. This sets the background to normal IT forensic analysis so that we can contrast it with forensic analysis of an Oracle database.

Types of Attack

Table 1-1 introduces a high-level list of some types of attack that could be performed against an Oracle database. This list includes a brief description of the attack type, the danger it poses to the owner of the data in the Oracle database, and the skill level needed to try the attack. This list is by no means exhaustive and in some cases an attack type may have multiple sub-types. For instance, SQL Injection could be SQL Injection of SQL code embedded in a remote PHP web application that accesses the database or it could be SQL injection of SQL code executed in a PL/SQL package in the database. It could even be SQL injection of SQL code in a batch process where the injection must be done via an INSERT statement.

There are many possible attack types and many of them can be combined into a single attack. This makes understanding how any particular attack took place difficult. There is no set list of rules that can be easily used to identify an attack.

The location of the attacker and the database is also very important to how the attack plays out. An attacker who is located internally to the business will more than likely have access to a desktop computer, probably with applications that access the database he wants to attack and possibly with tools that would allow a direct connection to the database. Most end users in an organization will probably not have credentials for the database; at least they may not understand if they do have credentials for the database. Some applications actually log into the database directly but the user enters the credentials in the screen of an application. Internally in an organization the staff is more likely to understand the data that is processed and possibly more likely to understand the architecture and technology used, therefore making an attack easier.

An external attack is much harder. If an attacker is able to exploit a publicly facing web site that serves its data from a database, then it may be possible to effectively tunnel your way in to the database. If this were not possible, then it would be much harder for an external attacker to gain access to an internal database. The attacker would first need to be able to get onto the network of the organization and then find a way to identify and access the database.

The list of attacks in Table 1-1 is not exhaustive and, as stated, an attacker could be internal or external and attacks can be combined. Factor in the multitude of operating system versions, Oracle database versions, and different types of applications, and you can see how each attack can look quite different.

Table 1-1. *Database Attack Types*

Attack Type	Danger	Skill Level	Description
SQL Injection	High/Low	High/Low	The danger is high or low depending on the data potentially exposed by the SQL that is attacked. The skill level is high or low depending on whether a tool can be used to perform the exploit.
Cross-Site Scripting	High/Low	High/Low	As with SQL injection, the danger depends on where the code that is exploited is located and what it does. Also the skill level depends again on whether an attacker can simply use a tool successfully or a manual attack is needed.
Payload Injection	High	High	The injection string must be first inserted as valid data for a trigger or later process to read it and place it into a SQL injection scenario.
DDL injection	High/Low	High/Low	Similar to SQL Injection.
PL/SQL Injection	High/Low	High/Low	Similar to SQL Injection.
DML Injection	High/Low	High/Low	Similar to SQL Injection.
Direct database access	High	Medium/High	Much harder, as the attacker needs IT skills and have to install a tool such as SQL*Plus, and would need to know at least Oracle TNS.

(*continued*)

Table 1-1. (*continued*)

Attack Type	Danger	Skill Level	Description
Data loss	High/Low	High/Low	This depends on how and where the data is stolen. Low would be an employee oimply stealing a paper report or printing a screen. High would be an attack against a web site and then working out how to target the data needed.
Escalation of database rights	High	High	An attacker would need direct database access via a tool such as SQL*Plus or an exploit in a web site that allows SQL or PL/SQL Injection that would allow DDL to be injected.
Access to operating system or network resources	High	High	An attacker would need elevated access to the database normally; then would need access to an account with OS or network access or would need skill to add the correct database objects.
Audit trail changes	High	High	An attacker would need elevated access to the database normally; then would need access to the audit trails or an account that has access
Audit settings changed	High	High	An attacker would need elevated access to the database normally; then would need access to the audit trail settings or an account that has access.

(*continued*)

Table 1-1. (*continued*)

Attack Type	Danger	Skill Level	Description
Security changes	High	High	An attacker would need elevated access to the database normally; then would need the ability to assess security settings and the ability to make changes.
Addition of database users	High	Medium/High	An attacker would need elevated direct access or access via a SQL injection that would allow DDL. This would be a highly skilled action done remotely.
Addition of database objects	High	Medium/High	An attacker would need elevated direct access or access via a SQL Injection that would allow DDL. This would be a highly skilled action done remotely.
Privilege highjack	High	High	An attacker would need access to make multiple queries to security settings and then the ability to change database objects.

A data breach could be carried out by a non-skilled person or a skilled person. In reality, it could be both. As part of forensic analysis that I have carried out, I noticed that with one customer system that was breached, a number of attack phases had occurred. From the analysis of the evidence that was gathered, it was clear that a number of different groups of attackers had been into this example system—some were clearly skilled, i.e., the target data was accessed swiftly, cleanly and with minimal steps. Other evidence showed completely unskilled, very noisy unsuccessful access attempts.

An Unskilled Breach

An *unskilled* breach can be likened to a thief who walks down a suburban street trying the doors of every car he passes to see if one is open, perhaps also giving windows a slight push to see if they are also open. This is opportunistic and unskilled. In terms of IT breaches against an Oracle database, unskilled attack could be an employee using a tool such as SQL*Plus or TOAD and attempting to guess passwords for every user account in the database. An example for an external attacker could be downloading a tool such as sqlmap (`http://sqlmap.org/`) and running it against a web site to see if the Oracle database supporting the web site can be exploited.

In general, an unskilled attack will look clumsy and noisy. By noisy, I mean a lot of errors and messages in the web server logs and database logs caused by thousands or even hundreds of thousands of actions pushed against the database.

An unskilled attack is generally the work of someone with very little skill with an Oracle database.

A Skilled Breach

A *skilled* attack, on the other hand, is finessed and in general much harder to detect. The attacker would be very skilled in gaining access to the database and also in locating and stealing the data that he needed. The attacker would take as few steps as possible, perhaps practicing on an external system not owned by the victim so as to work out the fewest actions possible to succeed.

A skilled breach would stand out by the lack of noise; skilled attacker would not simply run a brute force tool against the web site or database attempting to bully his way in. The skilled attacker may also use additional techniques to hide what they have done. They may delete audit records, log files, or other evidences that may point to their intrusion into the system.

The goal for a skilled attacker is to steal what he needs to steal, not for bragging rights. An unskilled attacker may escalate privileges simply to brag that he has done it, but a skilled attacker would take only the steps necessary to steal the data (if that were the target) and would not need to escalate his rights.

It is important when analyzing a potential breach to understand that the attack could have been random, brutal, and noisy, or it could have been stealthy. In other words, don't make the mistake of simply looking for noise in log files and then assuming the attack was not real if you don't find any.

What Is an Incident?

An *incident* is something that happens that is not normal or was not planned. This could be people (staff, outsiders, others) accessing data they are not authorized to see or making changes, or conversely, it could be making changes to the database structure or application code without a formal change control procedure.

Clearly in the context of this book, an incident can be one of many things but usually is attributed to an attacker. Don't make the mistake of assuming the attacker is some young kid in his bedroom hacking into your network and databases like Matthew Broderick in the film *WarGames* (`https://en.wikipedia.org/wiki/WarGames`). More than likely, the attacker is an employee.

It is an unfortunate fact that employees have much more knowledge of your systems than a kid in his bedroom. They will know where the valuable data is and they probably have a PC that you have provided them with applications, command-line tools, and more. Worst of all, you have probably gave them usernames and passwords to your systems. Of course, the attacker could also be external so you must not discount this possibility completely. Just don't discount the fact that an employee is in a much better position to steal from you.

An incident could be evidence that data is lost (data from your database has been located on Dropbox or Twitter or Facebook, for instance). It could be a change to security settings that was not authorized. It may be an indication that an attack is imminent rather than actually happened. The incident could also be an indication that an attack is in progress at the current time. The incident could also be a change to audit trails or settings or it could be that the change does not match any authorized change control release; indeed, an incident could be many things, but in general it is something that is not normal or authorized.

What is the difference between a data breach and an incident? I don't delve too deeply into technical definitions for the difference. A data breach is the technique, the method used to attack a database and steal data or do other things such as escalate privilege. An incident is the actual evidence for a specific instance of that data breach happening. The incident is the thing that you need to respond to, the data breach involves the actions taken by the attacker to break into the database.

What Is Incident Response?

Incident response is the process that is established to deal with a potential incident. This should include a documented plan of the actions to be taken should a incident or a potential incident occur. This should also include details of the team members who should be involved or who should be part of the team that will respond to the incident. It can also include details of tools and techniques to be used.

Your response to an incident must not be ad hoc. Incident response must be carefully planned in advance and must be a repeatable, reliable process. Chapter 3 discusses a sample incident response process in detail that you can use as a basis for your own incident response process in your organization.

What Is Forensic Analysis?

There are various definitions of forensics that can be found in dictionaries or indeed on the Internet. In general, forensics is the techniques used to analyze something, usually in the context of solving a crime. Forensics has become popular due to TV series such as CSI. In CSI, forensics is thought of as highly skilled, very detailed technical analysis of fragments of evidence to prove that somebody committed a crime. This is usually single hairs or strands of DNA or something equally tiny.

Forensic analysis can also be thought of as the argument to prove something. Often in the criminal world forensic evidence is carefully handled, documented, bagged, and presented as in court as provable and irrefutable evidence of a crime.

Therefore, forensic analysis is the process of looking at something, often in minute detail, together with a timeline of physical evidence that can be used to prove who the perpetrator of the crime was. This evidence must be able to stand up in court and not be thrown out. Sometimes in the criminal proceedings and expert may also be brought in to give expert opinion, perhaps to attest to the validity of the evidence in the context of the crime.

Chain of Custody

Traditional computer forensics tends to be focused on the analysis of personal computers and the evidence to be found on them. Most of the commercial tools available on the market are aimed at analyzing the hard disk of a PC. Forensics involves a number of steps. The first is the gathering of evidence; this is usually the seizure of a personal computer and its hard disk, perhaps the contents of someone's desk and notebooks. The analysis involves looking for computer evidence.

Evidence that could be presented in a court of law is usually one of four things:

- Real evidence

- Testimony

- Demonstration

- Documentation

Evidence in a computer case is usually real evidence or hard evidence; this is something you can physically pick up and carry and will be something that relates to the case in question. This could be an assailant's PC or the hard disk from his machine. It can also be files or programs stored on the machine. Computer evidence often also includes documentation, which again could be files, it can be printed paper. It could be notebooks or other written down or printed evidence.

In a criminal investigation, you need to often prove the identity and actions of the attacker. To do this, you must locate the actions in the real evidence; this could include URLs visited in a web server log or it could be a file that the assailant has downloaded and is currently still stored on his PC.

To prove the case in court, the investigator would need physical evidence to prove that the PC was used by the attacker. In the case of a PC that has been seized, this could be fingerprints on the actual system. In the case of data theft, this is harder to prove because most likely the attacker came across a network to the database to steal the data.

In an investigation, you need to be able to recognize what evidence to collect. This could be hardware or software or pieces of data files that will be useful to the investigation.

The process of evidence gathering and investigation should follow some basic steps and actions. These include the following:

- Before any physical evidence is touched, photograph it. Take photographs of the server, including its ID and serial numbers, and its location and cable connections. You may also photograph a place from where the attacker made the attack. If this was a DBA in your own organization, this could be his desk, his keyboard, his screen, and maybe the contents of his desk drawers.

- Ensure the legal requirements to access the system and to perform an investigation.

- Gather serial numbers and identifiers.

- Prepare proof that any tools you use does not corrupt any evidence that is gathered. This can be tough to do if you created the tools yourself. In one sense, it can be better to use pre-approved commercial tools that have already been used in legal cases and accepted in court.

- Prove the tools can be trusted in terms of providing the right answers. In other words, ensure the tools have not been modified to suit the attacker; i.e., to hide evidence.

- If necessary, remove the hard disk of the computer. In the case of a PC this is easy. In the case of a large Oracle system SAN or NAS storage, this is probably impossible. Checksum the disc and store the checksum securely. Copy the disk with software that makes a byte-to-byte copy. Checksum the copy and store the checksum securely. Compare the checksums to ensure they are identical. This ensures you have the physical one-to-one match of the disc for investigation

- Follow the chain of custody. Steps must be taken to ensure that the evidence that is collected is preserved and in pristine condition. Documentation must be kept that shows every step of movement of the evidence. This is called the chain of custody. Document all evidence and all actions against that evidence.

- For evidence to be admissible in court, there are two basic tenets to be applied. The first is that the evidence was legally obtained. The second is proof that the evidence has not been modified while it was in your possession. The chain of custody can be used to prove the second. The first must be checked and approved before the evidence is gathered.

- Integrity of data can be proved with checksums. These are normally cyclically redundancy checks (CRC) or MD5 checksums. These can be used on any piece of evidence, from a single file to a complete hard disk. This should be a standard method of any forensic investigation. We make checksums to ensure that we can prove the evidence collected is the same evidence when presented later and used in an analysis.

- Ensure that you create a collection and handling procedure and that all hardware is handled correctly. Ensure static electricity cannot damage the evidence and use a protected wrist strap. Figure 1-1 shows a photograph of a sample strap.

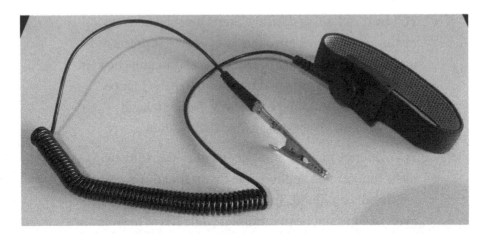

Figure 1-1. *A strap used to ensure static electricity cannot damage evidence. Copyright (c) 2017, PeteFinnigan.com Limited. Used with permission.*

- Some types of evidence, such as a PDA, require uninterrupted power to maintain the evidence in memory. The Oracle database has a similar issue with its SGA. If the power is removed from the database, all of the volatile data in the SGA is lost. A DBA can also issue a command to flush the shared pool, which will also remove the volatile data.

- If a case comes to court, you may need to prove that your investigation or incursion into a system did not change or corrupt anything. Again, checksum is a good tool to do this. Another method is to ensure that read-only access is used. In the PC world, right blocking hardware or software tools can be used to ensure that read-only access is made to a disc. In the Oracle world, this option doesn't present itself unless a disc that contains an Oracle database is analyzed statically in the same way as it would for a PC. To analyze an Oracle database, it's obviously much more advantageous to use an SQL interface to the database so you can more quickly and easily locate issues. But any access to the database is not read-only. This may make any incursion into the database inaccessible in court. By inference, any data that was obtained during this incursion into the database is not admissible.

- One method is to copy the system tablespace data file and treat it the same way as the analysis of a PC hard disk. Although this is not impossible, no tools exist to aid in this process. System tablespaces and the block structure inside of them are not documented fully; therefore, any analysis without using the database engine may also not be admissible in court because of the complexity of the structure and storage of data in the data dictionary. In general, a lot of evidence that would prove an attacker's actions in the database can be obtained from the data dictionary and not from the data itself. Adding users or procedures or dropping objects in the database will all be visible in the data dictionary, which is stored in the system tablespace.

- As another example, a copy of the SGA would be difficult to interpret outside of the Oracle database. The only way to do this is to do a memory dump from the server itself of the shared memory segments used by Oracle. To analyze this correctly, you need to know the complete structure of the so-called x$ tables used within the Oracle database. The SGA is made up of arrays of data structures. The x$ tables are not actually tables, but arrays of data in shared memory.

So although it's not impossible to analyze the SGA
outside of the database, it probably also would not be
admissible in court because there is no documentation
to prove that the access to the shared memory and its
local structure is correct.

The previous section discusses some of the main elements of forensic
analysis of IT systems. This usually means a PC. Contrasting a PC with an
Oracle database shows immediately that they are completely different. In
one sense, a PC is very simple and usually the evidence being searched for
is text files, documents, or images.

With an Oracle database, the evidence being searched for is the
investigation of data theft. Data theft does not actually remove the data
from the database and we are actually looking for evidence of someone
using the database engine to select that data. That evidence is tertiary
and complex and unless audit trails are enabled, it's usually missing. So
periphery or correlating evidence usually is the target. For instance, the
attacker must log in to show evidence that this connection happened.
The attacker may have entered a SELECT query and the Oracle optimizer
gets involved with a compilation of the SQL and in some cases it stores
evidence of predicates in a dictionary database table. If the attack is
investigated very quickly, then the SQL used by the attacker may be
present in the SGA. If the attack came from a web server, then perhaps the
SQL is available in the web server logs application server logs.

Analyzing an Oracle database is much easier if you can use the Oracle
database to perform the analysis. Because the structure of the Oracle
database is not fully documented and is very complex, using SQL as a tool
is much simpler.

The same basic rules that apply when analyzing a PC apply when
analyzing an Oracle database, but it's different. Another issue to bear in
mind with an Oracle database is the issue of licensing. If a server that runs
Oracle database is taken in as evidence and then that server is copied in the

traditional manner, then effectively a copy of the Oracle database has been created. Oracle would be due an additional license fee for this additional database. Before using traditional methods, Oracle database licensing must be considered. Another example is using the tuning pack and diagnostic pack to analyze any historic SQL that appear in the database; again, this method would require payment of an additional license. The Investigator of an Oracle database must remember to consider the legality of accessing the database even after the investigation has legally begun.

Listing 1-1 shows a sample usage of the DBMS_SQLHASH package to checksum the source code of itself. This sample satisfies two requirements. It demonstrates the use of the built-in package in the database to easily create checksums of objects within the database and it also demonstrates checking the validity of the hash package itself. The hash that's generated can be compared to a hash from a similar clean database.

Listing 1-1. Create a SHA1 Checksum of the DBMS_SQLHASH Package

```
SQL> select sys.dbms_sqlhash.gethash('select text from
dba_source where name=''DBMS_SQLHASH''',3) from dual;

SYS.DBMS_SQLHASH.GETHASH('SELECTTEXTFROMDBA_
SOURCEWHERENAME=''DBMS_SQLHASH''',3)
----------- ---------------------------------------------------
------------------
3ED360B4B98C9F6B762B4629D3B609E580424021

SQL>
```

This example seems to show an easy way to validate that the DBMS_SQLHASH package in the database being investigated has not been compromised by the attacker. The problem is that it's not as simple as this. Listing 1-2 shows the dependencies used by the DBMS_SQLHASH package.

Listing 1-2. Dependencies on the DBMS_SQLHASH Package

```
SQL> col referenced_name for a12
SQL> col referenced_owner for a10
SQL> col referenced_type for a10
SQL> select referenced_name, referenced_owner, referenced_type
  2  from dba_dependencies
  3  where owner='SYS' and name='DBMS_SQLHASH';

REFERENCED_N REFERENCED REFERENCED
------------ ---------- ----------
STANDARD     SYS        PACKAGE
STANDARD     SYS        PACKAGE
UTL_RAW      SYS        PACKAGE
DBMS_LOB     SYS        PACKAGE
DBMS_SQL     SYS        PACKAGE
DBMS_CRYPTO  SYS        PACKAGE
DBMS_SQLHASH SYS        PACKAGE

7 rows selected.

SQL>
```

To properly validate that DBMS_SQLHASH has not been modified,
you would also need to obtain checksums of UTL_RAW, DBMS_LOB, and
DBMS_CRYPTO. But the problem doesn't stop there—you would then need
to run the same dependency query to see which other packages depend
on these three packages. You would then need to do the same thing again
and again for any child dependencies of those. To be thorough, you should
also obtain a checksum of the view used to test for the dependencies and
any dependencies on that view. As you can see, validating the source
of evidence and the tools used in an Oracle database can be extremely
complex. Prepared checksums of all of these elements would also need to

be obtained from a known clean database. How do you prove that another database is clean?

What Is Oracle Database Forensics?

Forensic analysis in the context of Oracle security and the Oracle database is very new. Although data breaches are very common and reported regularly on national news channels news, detailed forensic analysis of a breach of a specific Oracle database is unreported and unknown. I have been involved in the forensic analysis of quite a number of Oracle databases since 2004.

Oracle forensics is the process by which someone (an auditor?) tries to determine when/how/why and by who something happened. The techniques gather and correlate incriminating evidence from the Oracle database. In this context, Oracle forensics often occurs when, as an auditor, the author is called in to help a client discover how a breach occurred and hopefully some clue as to who did it. The techniques used are often limited by two factors:

- The client finds out that their database has been breached weeks and often months after the actual breach, so there is no transient or current data in the database to use as evidence.

- There is no audit trail enabled for the database.

These two factors make it very difficult to establish exactly what happened and when and the results of each investigation are dependent on these two factors.

Oracle forensics should be considered as the same as forensics of physical evidence, but we must also consider the size of Oracle databases and the need to keep an Oracle database running so businesses can continue without interruption. Analysis of the PC in comparison to an

Oracle database is much simpler for two reasons. The first is that a PC is much smaller and simpler than an Oracle database and second is often the analysis of a PC is searching for images or text. The Oracle database, although it stores its data in files exactly the same as a PC, is much more complex.

If an Oracle forensics investigation leads to criminal proceedings, the evidence must be gathered without distortion or change to the system. Otherwise, the evidence might not be acceptable for use in court.

How Does Oracle Function and Store Data?

Understanding how Oracle works is helpful for any future forensic analysis. This knowledge will allow you to locate evidence or artifacts that are relevant to any incident response. Figure 1-2 shows a high-level overview of some of the elements of the Oracle database that are involved with processing SQL statements. This description is not meant to be a finite detailed analysis that perhaps would be used in text describing a tuning problem. The purpose of this description is simply to highlight how Oracle stores and caches useful pieces of information. Keep in mind the high-level nature of the description.

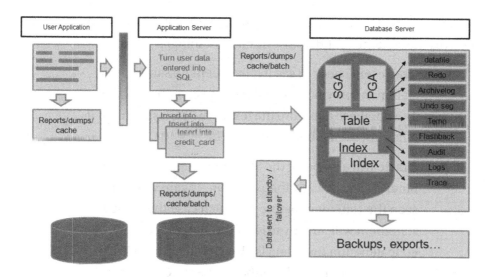

Figure 1-2. *High-level view of how Oracle works (c)Copyright 2017. PeteFinnigan.com Limited. Used with permission.*

Figure 1-2 can be read from left to right to show the processing of a typical user entering data in an application. The data is transported to the database and used to query or insert information and update data in the same database.

In this example, the user enters data in the fields of the user application shown at the top left of Figure 1-2. The application could be web-based or forms based or indeed any other type of application. In this example, the web application sends the entered data—perhaps this is a first name, last name, or a credit card number—through a firewall to an application server. The application server receives this data and converts it into a SQL statements. These statements could be SELECT, INSERT, UPDATE, or DELETE. The statements could also simply concatenate the data received into the SQL statement or it could use prepared statements or bind variables. This SQL statement is then sent to the database. The database receives the statement and does a number of things:

- Oracle will check to see if it has seen the same statement previously by taking a hash of the SQL text. The database will store the text of the SQL statement if it has not seen it before in the SGA.

- Oracle will also parse the SQL statement and create a binary version ready for execution—again unless it has seen the statement before, in which case the parsed statement will already exist. If the statement uses concatenation then data is also stored in the SGA, for instance a credit card number. If the statement uses bind variables then the bind variables are separated and stored separately in the SGA.

The database will then execute the statement, which involves bringing blocks of data from the data files into the SGA. Because of the way Oracle works, it will not bring back a single record that is required for a SELECT statement, but it may bring back multiple blocks, each of which may contain hundreds of records. If critical information involved in the statement is also part of an index column, then index data will also be read into the SGA. The Oracle database's ability to be highly available and highly resilient means that undo and redo are generated. These are also stored initially in the SGA in a transient way. The redo is also committed to a redo log file on a periodic basis and also to archive log files. The undo allows a transaction to be rolled back. The redo allows a record to be reapplied, such as in the case of a recovery scenario.

The Oracle database is also very heavily instrumented. The database allows customers to request dumps of data files, the redo log, archive log, the SGA, and many more elements of the database structure. Customers also can set events or traces that log actions to the trace file in the event of a certain event happening, perhaps an Oracle error. In some circumstances, the database may also automatically generate trace files if an error occurs.

If database auditing is enabled, then this will also record the relevant actions to an audit log. The audit log can be stored to the database, to the operating system, or to syslog in 11g and 12c, if mixed mode auditing is enabled. In 12c, if unified audit is enabled, then the audit trail is written to the unified audit trail.

The Oracle database may also employ data guard or similar technology to replicate the database in a real or semi-real mode to another database. Again, this is for availability and resilience. Finally, the customer could or indeed should back up the database using Oracle's RMAN tool or make cold backups.

This brief description shows that data and actions are replicated throughout the database. The SQL statements that are issued from an application are stored as partial text or full text in the SGA as well as bind variables.

The SGA is transient, so the data held in it is held for a limited amount of time, but this is not fixed. Statements age out of the SGA depending on how often they are used, so very frequently used statements stay in the SGA almost permanently and statements rarely used age out fairly quickly.

Redo logs and archive logs are a useful source of changes that have occurred in the database both to data and to structure. For instance, when creating a new PL/SQL procedure. The audit trail is obvious; it should record an audit record for all of the actions that it has been configured to capture. Trace files and log files can also contain SQL statements and data. As databases are replicated, it is also possible that changes can be extracted at the same time. Copies of databases that are perhaps taken for use in test and development systems will more than likely be copies on a less regular basis than replication. For instance, a database may be copied once a week and replenished in a test system. This means a test system is a good source for comparison against the production system.

This section highlights the fact that Oracle does store evidence of some actions in different parts of the database log files and these can be very useful for forensic analysis. This means that an Oracle practitioner who wants to perform incident response of forensic analysis knowing how the database works and knowing where it places artifacts is very important.

Oracle 12c Multitenant

Since Oracle version 12.1.0.1, Oracle has supported a drastically different architecture. Oracle created the concept of multitenant databases, where a single root container database can contain multiple pluggable databases. Since version 12.2.0.1, this concept went even further to allow application pluggable containers held in an application root. The application root can be thought of as a pluggable container in the root container and it can contain any number of application containers, which of course can be thought of as pluggable containers. This creates a complex hierarchy of databases.

In simplest terms, each pluggable database is intended to have the look and feel of a legacy single instance database. So all scripts, tools, and views in the database should respond in exactly the same way as though they were a single database.

Oracle still allows a 12c database to be installed in legacy mode; in other words, a single instance database that could be installed in version 11g. In legacy mode, quite obviously a 12c database has the look and feel of an 11g database, but this mode was deprecated at the start of 12c. This means all customers should be moving toward multitenant architecture with at least a single pluggable tenant.

Multitenant architecture intends to make the database feel the same as a 11g. Although this is comforting, there is still effectively a second database to consider for every single pluggable database that is the root container.

Because multitenant architecture shares resources between the root container and all pluggable containers of tenants, you must consider these factors in a forensic investigation. In general, Oracle has tried, very well in fact, to separate resources in the context of the pluggable database. However, if someone were logged into the root container, they can see everything across the root container and all the pluggable tenants. This is either because some privileges and code and views are common or because someone with access to the root container as a common user can log into or switch sessions to a pluggable tenant.

As part of forensic analysis of the 12c database that includes multitenant architecture, you must establish where the breach occurred. Did it occur in a single pluggable database, were other pluggable databases in the same container affected, or did the breach occur in the root container? If the breach occurred in the root container, did the attacker then access each pluggable container?

The concepts and ideas presented in this book should be considered as a single tenant level initially. So, in other words, perform the analysis in the pluggable database or the root container where the breach is known to have occurred. After standard analysis considering the root container or the pluggable tenant as a single instance database has been completed, factor in the multitenant issues that the attacker could have accessed other tenant databases of the root container itself.

CHAPTER 2

Artifacts

Many dictionary definitions of artifact state that it is usually something made by human being and is typically important. An artifact can also be something observed in science that is not naturally present.

Artifacts and pieces of information that we would like to extract from the database or the operating system or the web servers or the log files that will help us understand what may have happened in the database. Collecting artifacts may alter the database, so we will explore this issue first before looking at the different types of artifacts that we can collect at the database level and from outside of the database—the non-database level. The database level artifacts can be further broken down into two groups. The first are those that relate to transient data. Oracle caches a lot of information in its SGA and uses it to maintain the speed, efficiency and reliability of the database, but this data changes often and fast. The second type of database artifact are the records stored in the database.

Time and identity are also very important in terms of artifact collection and forensic analysis. We are interested in time for a number of reasons, the first being that we need to ensure all the records that contain a timestamp from different sources are actually all aligned with each other. Leading on from this we also want to ensure that we can lay out all of the information we collect in sequential order so that we can see the actions performed by the attacker in the correct sequence. Identity is also important, because if we cannot identify who actually performed in action in the database then we cannot determine easily how the attack played out.

© Pete Finnigan 2018
P. Finnigan, *Oracle Incident Response and Forensics*,
https://doi.org/10.1007/978-1-4842-3264-4_2

Correlation of data is obviously incredibly important, and some elements when combined may give enough information to tell a story, yet on their own they have less value.

One of the biggest problems with analyzing an Oracle database for forensic issues unless audit is enabled is that we cannot detect read statements easily for the access of any data. If audit is enabled, for instance for the credit card table, then we can detect reading against the credit card table, but if audit is not enabled, this becomes incredibly difficult, in fact almost impossible. In that case, we are relegated to looking for tertiary evidence of actions the attacker may have taken that relate to his goal of reading data.

David Litchfield has written much over 10 years ago on the subject of detecting deleted data in an Oracle database. Most of this research related to using techniques used by others in tools used to extract data from a destroyed database many years previous to that. In fact, it's rare for Oracle to actually delete any data; it instead marks each record with a single bit to show that it's deleted. This data no longer shows up in SQL statements, but it is still there at the datafile level. A reasonably sound investigation can use tools provided by the Oracle database to read redo logs or archive logs, which also contain a record of all changes to the database.

We close the chapter with a brief look at *rootkits*. These are tools installed by an attacker to hide his presence and potentially to allow him to gain access again in the future. A rootkit could hamper an investigation.

Heisenberg's Uncertainty Principle of Oracle

Werner Heisenberg was one of the key people involved in the pioneering of quantum mechanics in the first quarter of the 20th Century. Heisenberg defined a method to devise quantum mechanics as matrices, he was awarded the Nobel Prize for physics in 1932 for this. In 1927, while working at Niels Bohrs research lab, Heisenberg formulated his uncertainty principle. Heisenberg's uncertainty principle states:

> It is impossible to simultaneously know the exact position and momentum of a particle. The more exactly the position of a particle is known, then less is known of the momentum. The more exactly the momentum is known, the less exactly the position is known.

Although an Oracle database does not work at the quantum level, we have a very similar issue with forensic analysis. Because of the way Oracle works whenever forensic analysis is performed in general, it will alter the database. Put simply, almost anything you do to the database changes the database. The change can vary depending on the action performed. For instance, selecting data from a table will modify the SGA as the SQL text, the parsed text, cursors, and many more settings are stored in the SGA. The database is not static, particularly the transient data such as that stored in the SGA.

Clearly reading evidence from a compromised database must be done very carefully and in the correct order so that the database is not modified in such a way that it would render any further forensic evidence invalid. The data that is more likely to change must be extracted first. Chapter 4 discusses this in more detail in the "Live Artifact Collection" section.

Audit Trail or No Audit Trail?

One of the most important artifacts that we want to use in an incident response and forensic analysis of an Oracle database are audit trail entries. These entries are specifically set up to capture certain events in the database; such as adding a user, changing a password, and accessing a specific table of records in the database.

Even if audit trails are enabled and exist, quite often they will not be detailed enough or capture the relevant actions to give a very clear picture of what happened in an attack. Even worse, the problem is that when you want to investigate why the attack took place, there is inevitably very little or no audit trail.

The audit trail is very important so if it is available then we can certainly use elements of it; if not it makes our task much harder. Chapter 6 highlights the need to design practical and sophisticated audit trails for your database so that the future incidents audit trails are available and are useful.

Be aware of also testing any existing audit trail as part of an analysis to make sure that that audit trail has not been altered. This is one of the key tenets of forensics analysis; the so-called chain of custody. Detecting if the audit trail has been altered without additional audit is again difficult. Oracle provides facilities to allow "audits of audits," which is covered in Chapter 6.

If there is no audit then it is still possible to rely on redo logs or archive logs to capture the changes made to the database. If redo or archive logs are not available then this makes the task much harder. All is not lost, as there are still some possibilities to capture evidence—tuning views, stats back, secondary evidence.

Performing forensic analysis is made easier when there is a very detailed audit trail available that has captured all of the actions performed by the attacker. Often in the authors experience there is very little audit trail and it usually does not capture the actions necessary to analyze the current issue.

The Problem of Detecting READ

One of the biggest issues for forensic analysis of an Oracle database is that the database does not normally record read access to anything. In almost all cases, changes to the database, such as updates, inserts, and deletes of data including application tables and dictionary tables are recorded.

This is whether the audit trail is enabled or not. Changes are recorded in redo and archive logs and in some cases changes can be gleaned from dictionary tables by analyzing the records. If an attack can be detected while it is ongoing or very soon afterward, then read activity may be visible in the SGA.

One of the key attacks that we see reported in the national press is data theft. This is reading of data. This means that one of the biggest groups of attacks as far as the press is concerned is reading of data. Naturally, we would like the database to record this read activity, but it doesn't.

The only way to be sure that access to certain data is captured for read is to pre-enable audit trails on that data. In reality, even a read based attack—an attack that steals data—will probably include other elements. Perhaps the attacker is unskilled and perhaps he uses noisy tools that generate a web server level in the database level. Even though the specific read actions are not captured some of the periphery actions will be.

Identity and Accountability

Analysis of various artifacts in the database or an external log files such as a web server may provide evidence to prove that the attack occurred but one additional element is always needed—*identity*. Without identity there is no accountability. Without a doubt, identity is one of the most important elements of the analysis. Each action that is captured must be attributable to a real person. It may be an individual groups of records cannot be attributed to a real person but combined with other elements perhaps they can. For instance a web server log may attribute an IP address with a real person. The attacker perhaps injects SQL through a web site and makes a change to the database. The records in the database are attributed to the user used to connect the application server to the database. If the end user's attributes are not transferred into the database, then it's not possible to directly attribute an action in the database with a real person.

It is possible, through correlation of records where one set of records can be directly related to another in a different part of the system, to prove who actually executed them.

It is important to ensure all artifacts extracted from the database either have an accountable field included with them, such as a user ID, machine name, and IP address, or at least they can be linked to additional records that do include this type of information. Effort must be made during capture and analysis to think about accountability and identity

Time

Time comes into play in three different ways:

- **Correlation of timestamps across different systems and targets**: It is important to establish a correlation of timestamps across all the systems that are part of the analysis. This includes Oracle databases, operating systems of the servers that support the Oracle database, web servers, client computers, and more. Often even in an organization where NTP is used there is a discrepancy between the timestamps of each of the machines. Although we may not be working to a millisecond or microsecond accuracy, one of the goals of the analysis is to time order all of the artifacts or records that we are able to extract from the systems that could be part of the attack. It must be established if there is a significant time difference between each of the systems so that all of the time-based artifacts can be correctly aligned and synchronized. Also ensure that the wall time (the current time by an accurate wall clock) is also synchronized with each of the systems.

- **Establish the timeslot of the attack**: This is very difficult to do because initially we don't even know what the attack looks like or if it really even happened. We need to establish a start date and an end date for the potential attack. The end date scenario is now or the time of the beginning of the analysis of the attack. The start time of the attack is much harder to establish; in my experience as the forensic analyst and security auditor, the client often has a specific point in time when they know an attack has happened. This is often the appearance of some of their data that can be proved to have come from their production database on a public web site such as Dropbox. But subsequent analysis of the customer's database often reveals that the attack occurred or started much earlier. So in summary, you need to establish a start date and an end date for the potential breach but you should be flexible to move the start date backwards as the analysis progresses.

- **Time within the database**: There are many Oracle dictionary views and tables that contain date or timestamp columns. A naive search of an Oracle 12.2.0.1 database shows 4710 such columns in the data dictionary owned by SYS. A similar search of other default users of the Oracle database and of application tables and views will also reveal many such columns. Clearly, it's not possible to search 4,710 dictionary views in every analysis, as this would be severely impacting. The existence of so much time-based data should be noted and can be used as part of any analysis.

Database Artifacts

The Oracle data dictionary is complex and large, so is not possible to cover every possible artifact that could be collected from the data dictionary as part of forensic analysis. Instead we will focus on high-level groups of artifacts that can be extracted from the database so that you can use this information to explore in more depth if necessary. Examples will be given for each main area where appropriate. You can extend the ideas presented in the section and extract more or fewer artifacts from the database if necessary.

Database artifacts are records or information that can be extracted from within the database that may prove useful as part of forensic analysis. These will include data that reflects SQL statements, changes to objects, changes to records, dumps from the database, and many more.

This section discusses the possible artifacts at a high level and in a general way. Chapter 4 will look at artifact collection again in a specific way in the discussion around responding to a specific incident. In Chapter 4, we look to extract artifact details from target database that has been attacked. Chapter 5 discusses the forensic analysis of the extracted data to try and establish how the attack took place and as much detail as possible about it.

Chapter 4 also discusses some of the constraints and issues around artifact collection. The discussion here is more general to give you an overview of the types of data that could be pulled from the database and some general examples.

Tables or Views with SQL

One area of immense interest to a forensic analyst is to establish if any of the SQL statements that have been issued to the database can be extracted and used in an investigation. As stated earlier, by default Oracle does not capture or audit READ or SELECT statements. The only chance you have

to establish evidence of a READ within the database is to look for SQL
statements that can possibly be assigned back to an attacker.

There are many views within the database that include SQL text.
Listing 2-1 shows a simple query against an Oracle 12.2.0.1 database
to locate many of these possible locations. This is a naive search as we
assume that a column in a table or view containing SQL text has the words
SQL and text in its name. If Oracle stores SQL text in a different name
column, this query will not find it; so there may be other tables or views
available.

Listing 2-1. A Simple Query to Locate SQL Text

```
SQL> select table_name
  2  from dba_tab_columns
  3  where column_name like '%SQL%TEXT%'
  4  and owner='SYS';

TABLE_NAME
-----------------------------------------------------------
BOOTSTRAP$
PDB_SYNC_STMT$
JIREFRESHSQL$
SQLTXL_SOL$
SQL$TEXT
PLSCOPE_SQL$
PLSCOPE_SQL$
AUD$
FGA_LOG$
FGA_LOG$
V_$SQL_REDIRECTION
```

```
TABLE_NAME
-----------------------------------------------------------
V_$SQLAREA
V_$SQLAREA
V_$SQLAREA_PLAN_HASH
V_$SQLAREA_PLAN_HASH
V_$SQLTEXT
V_$SQLTEXT_WITH_NEWLINES
V_$SQL
V_$SQL
V_$OPEN_CURSOR

...
```

Some of these views of tables are not relevant such as BOOTSTRAP$, which contains the bootstrap DDL used when the database starts up. This is not SQL that an attacker has issued. In Oracle 12.2.0.1 locates 125 possible places that SQL may exist. Early versions of Oracle will return fewer rows.

The key views that we are interested in are VSQL, VSQLAREA, V$SQLTEXT, and V$SQLTEXT_WITH_NEWLINES. Each of these views has different structure but clearly references the same data. V$SQL shows all SQL for all queries that are currently captured in the SGA. V$SQLAREA contains an aggregate of the previous view. So, for instance, if user U1 has submitted select * from someview and user U2 has also submitted select * from someview against the same name view but in his own schema, then V$SQL will show both SQL statements, but the aggregate will show only one. Listing 2-2 shows the detail available in this view from one sample record.

Listing 2-2. Details of a Record in V$SQL

```
SQL> set serveroutput on
SQL> @print 'select * from v$sql'
old  33:          --lv_str:=translate('&&1','''','''''');
```

```
new   33:          --lv_str:=translate('select * from
v$sql','''','''''');
old   34:          print('&&1');
new   34:          print('select * from v$sql');
Executing Query [select * from v$sql]
...
SQL_TEXT                          : select sql_text from v$sqltext
SQL_FULLTEXT                      : select sql_text from v$sqltext
SQL_ID                           : chq1fpupmo3dw
SHARABLE_MEM                      : 35575
PERSISTENT_MEM                    : 4088
RUNTIME_MEM                       : 2760
SORTS                            : 0
LOADED_VERSIONS                   : 1
OPEN_VERSIONS                     : 0
USERS_OPENING                     : 0
FETCHES                          : 7190
EXECUTIONS                        : 1
PX_SERVERS_EXECUTIONS             : 0
END_OF_FETCH_COUNT                : 1
USERS_EXECUTING                   : 0
LOADS                            : 1
FIRST_LOAD_TIME                   : 2017-06-07/13:30:51
INVALIDATIONS                     : 0
PARSE_CALLS                       : 1
DISK_READS                        : 0
DIRECT_WRITES                     : 0
DIRECT_READS                      : 0
BUFFER_GETS                       : 6
APPLICATION_WAIT_TIME             : 0
CONCURRENCY_WAIT_TIME             : 0
```

CLUSTER_WAIT_TIME   : 0
USER_IO_WAIT_TIME   : 0
PLSQL_EXEC_TIME   : 0
JAVA_EXEC_TIME   : 0
ROWS_PROCESSED   : 14377
COMMAND_TYPE   : 3
OPTIMIZER_MODE   : ALL_ROWS
OPTIMIZER_COST   : 1
OPTIMIZER_ENV   :

E289FB892169B7002D020000AEF9C3E2CFFA3310564145555519521105545
55154554555859155544
9665851D551105855555515551512255415A0EA0C5551454265455454449
081566E001696C6A355
451501025415504416FD557151551555551001550A16214545D1C35444A1
C11015595510250150335
5555555551E91F1411855B0501655D564561405515256 45001F9A456016
885A4DD02140808000008
0000004000000004000080000008 20401F0000000028 0000800C0004040000
E0E03F0A0000004006
000000140084A4DD02949191090890C908C8000008000C082828141428500
0080000D00700009029
28282890A10F00009001030E0800080000FCFF03001008C80001000100A00
F0000409C0000008000
0028780C2003002000000400004 09C00000C1000200000042A005A6202A00
F00002C91FDFF0300FC
FF03000040000050801A06009001813801001C0820238FF8FF0300FCF
F030008100001
OPTIMIZER_ENV_HASH_VALUE   : 1192275068
PARSING_USER_ID   : 0
PARSING_SCHEMA_ID   : 0
PARSING_SCHEMA_NAME   : SYS

```
KEPT_VERSIONS                  : 0
ADDRESS                        : 0000000061C35670
TYPE_CHK_HEAP                  : 00
HASH_VALUE                     : 2872053180
OLD_HASH_VALUE                 : 2234513503
PLAN_HASH_VALUE                : 1787836842
FULL_PLAN_HASH_VALUE           : 1586957109
CHILD_NUMBER                   : 0
SERVICE                        : orcl.localdomain
SERVICE_HASH                   : 0
MODULE                         : sqlplus.exe
MODULE_HASH                    : 254292535
ACTION                         :
ACTION_HASH                    : 0
SERIALIZABLE_ABORTS            : 0
OUTLINE_CATEGORY               :
CPU_TIME                       : 35000
ELAPSED_TIME                   : 224549
OUTLINE_SID                    :
CHILD_ADDRESS                  : 0000000080E6D7B0
SQLTYPE                        : 6
REMOTE                         : N
OBJECT_STATUS                  : VALID
LITERAL_HASH_VALUE             : 0
LAST_LOAD_TIME                 : 2017-06-07/13:30:51
IS_OBSOLETE                    : N
IS_BIND_SENSITIVE              : N
IS_BIND_AWARE                  : N
IS_SHAREABLE                   : Y
CHILD_LATCH                    : 0
SQL_PROFILE                    :
```

```
SQL_PATCH                        :
SQL_PLAN_BASELINE                :
PROGRAM_ID                       : 0
PROGRAM_LINE#                    : 0
EXACT_MATCHING_SIGNATURE         : 17475387565425291141
FORCE_MATCHING_SIGNATURE         : 17475387565425291141
LAST_ACTIVE_TIME                 : 20170607133115
BIND_DATA                        :
TYPECHECK_MEM                    : 0
IO_CELL_OFFLOAD_ELIGIBLE_BYTES: 0
IO_INTERCONNECT_BYTES            : 0
PHYSICAL_READ_REQUESTS           : 0
PHYSICAL_READ_BYTES              : 0
PHYSICAL_WRITE_REQUESTS          : 0
PHYSICAL_WRITE_BYTES             : 0
OPTIMIZED_PHY_READ_REQUESTS      : 0
LOCKED_TOTAL                     : 1
PINNED_TOTAL                     : 2
IO_CELL_UNCOMPRESSED_BYTES       : 0
IO_CELL_OFFLOAD_RETURNED_BYTES: 0
CON_ID                           : 0
IS_REOPTIMIZABLE                 : N
IS_RESOLVED_ADAPTIVE_PLAN        :
IM_SCANS                         : 0
IM_SCAN_BYTES_UNCOMPRESSED       : 0
IM_SCAN_BYTES_INMEMORY           : 0
DDL_NO_INVALIDATE                : N
IS_ROLLING_INVALID               : N
IS_ROLLING_REFRESH_INVALID       : N    ...
```

This view also shows a lot of relevant details of the SQL being executed such as the last date it was active. We can gain knowledge of the user who executed and parsed the query. Be careful with this, as some SQL is executed in the background as SYS when other SQL is executed. The output shows the last time the SQL statement was used, the last time it was loaded (presumably into the SQL virtual machine), and the program used—sqlplus.exe. It shows the first time it was loaded and how many times it was loaded. Most importantly, it shows the actual SQL.

The disadvantage of the SGA is that a database restart flushes it, and a manual shared pool flush will also remove evidence. The data is very transient in that there are limited rows of data available and the space is reused by Oracle fairly quickly.

A number of the views returned in Listing 2-2 are for tuning and diagnostic pack related data. Be aware that accessing these views requires an additional license.

Tables or Views with Bind Data

A number of tables or views in the database also hold bind data. Bind data is the data entered by an end user that is bound to an SQL statement, such as select * from sometable where name=:name, where :name is a bind variable and its contents are replaced by data entered at execution time.

A simple query such as select table_name from dba_tab_columns where column_name like '%BIND%' and owner='SYS'; and select view_name from dba_views where view_name like '%BIND%' will show tables and views in the database that possibly contain bind data. One of the views of particular interest returned from these queries is V$SQL_BIND_CAPTURE. Listing 2-3 shows sample output from this view.

Listing 2-3. Sample Output from v$sql_bind_capture

```
SQL> col sql_id for 999999
SQL> col datatype for 99
SQL> col last_captured for a14
SQL> col value_string for a100
```

```
SQL> set lines 220
SQL> select sql_id,datatype,last_captured,value_string
  2  from v$sql_bind_capture;
SQL_ID          DATATYPE LAST_CAPTURED  VALUE_STRING
-------------- -------- -------------- ------------------------
2wdrw5tqputaq         2 20170607012844 75970
crmdt678jathx         1 20170607002834 NULL
crmdt678jathx         1 20170607002834 SYS
crmdt678jathx         1 20170607002834 WRI$_HEATMAP_TOP_TABLESPACES
crmdt678jathx         1 20170607002834 NULL
crmdt678jathx         1 20170607002834 SYS
crmdt678jathx         1 20170607002834 WRI$_HEATMAP_TOP_TABLESPACES
crmdt678jathx         1 20170607013846 NULL
crmdt678jathx         1 20170607013846 SYS
crmdt678jathx         1 20170607013846 WRI$_HEATMAP_TOP_TABLESPACES
crmdt678jathx         1 20170607013846 NULL
...
```

Note that bind data available on this view could be stored as text or it could be stored as the Oracle ANYDATA value that's not shown here. If bind data of interest is located with this view, then the analyst should try to link the SQL ID or hash with all the records in the database to try to establish where the bind data was used.

Tables or Views with Timestamps

The Oracle data dictionary is huge and complex and many of its tables and views include columns that record date or timestamp records. Any of these records can potentially be useful in a forensic analysis. Listing 2-4 shows a simplistic search of the database for any table or view that has a column that is a date or timestamp.

Listing 2-4. A Search for Time and Date Stamps in the Database

```
SQL> col owner for a20
SQL> col table_name for a30
SQL> col column_name for a30
SQL> col data_type for a30
SQL> set lines 220
SQL> select owner,table_name,column_name,data_type
  2  from dba_tab_columns
  3  where data_type='DATE' or data_type like 'TIMESTAMP%';

...
SYS       USER_USERS      LOCK_DATE       DATE
SYS       USER_USERS      EXPIRY_DATE     DATE
SYS       USER_USERS      CREATED         DATE
SYS       DBA_USERS       LOCK_DATE       DATE
SYS       DBA_USERS       EXPIRY_DATE     DATE
SYS       DBA_USERS       CREATED         DATE
SYS       DBA_USERS       LAST_LOGIN      TIMESTAMP(9) WITH TIME ZONE
SYS       CDB_USERS       LOCK_DATE       DATE
SYS       CDD_USERS       EXPIRY_DATE     DATE
SYS       CDB_USERS       CREATED         DATE

OWNER     TABLE_NAME      COLUMN_NAME     DATA_TYPE
------    -------------   -------------   ---------------------------
SYS       CDB_USERS       LAST_LOGIN      TIMESTAMP(9) WTTH TIME ZONE
...
4848 rows selected.

SQL>
```

This query in Oracle 12.2.0.1 returns almost 5,000 individual columns that may contain time information. Using timestamps on the object that you are investigating, for instance user accounts or procedures, is very useful on two levels. First, the creation or update of a particular object can be confirmed to have occurred during the known timescale of the attack. Second, if some piece of evidence is found that can be attributed to the attacker, then all other objects in the database that could potentially be involved can also be linked by testing the timestamp audit columns to see if any change or insertion of records occurred during the same timeframe or even at the same timestamp.

Using timestamps to create a timeline of events is one of the core tenets of forensics analysis.

A timestamp or a date column is unfortunately not going to be useful if the action by the attacker was deletion. Different techniques, such as looking for deleted data in a datafile using redo log analysis, may be helpful in this case.

Privilege Changes

A key indication of part of an attack may be changes to privileges within the database. An attacker may seek to grant himself membership of powerful roles or may seek to grant himself system privileges or object privileges (grants to execute procedures or grants to select from tables for instance).

Detecting these actions at a high level in the database is harder because none of the key views that store information of privileges such as:

```
DBA_TAB_PRIVS
DBA_SYS_PRIVS
DBA_ROLE_PRIVS
```

And even the base table

```
SYS.SYSAUTH$
```

Include any date or timestamp columns. The change to privilege in the Oracle database is therefore not natively captured as a timestamp. There are still methods to obtain changes to privilege. One method would be to use the flashback functionality, if enabled in the database, and compare the current privileges to those of a time in the past. The time in the past should initially be just before the start of the attack, as this will confirm if any additional privileges were added during the attack that haven't been deleted. More detailed checks can be made throughout the attack with a comparison to the current time to try to detect if any privileges were added and then removed during the attack.

If test systems exist that are populated from the production database, a comparison can also be made between those test systems and the current state of the production system that was attacked.

The analyst can also look at the system tablespace datafile for deleted records that relate to the SYS.SYSAUTH$ table to see if any privilege records were removed. A cursory check against the three main views can be made simply by listing the contents of these reviews and checking for any privileges that do not look consistent with the normal operation of the database.

Finally, LogMiner could also be used to analyze redo changes.

Changes to Security

An attacker may also attempt to modify any security controls that you enabled in your database. This could include hardening elements such as database initialization parameters. It can also include data access controls, user privilege controls, or password management. Changes to security can also include attempts to modify context-based security. Context-based security is where security is enabled based on the current situation of the logged-in user. This is popular with Oracle additional cost options such as Virtual Private database, Oracle label security, and database vault. These tools depend on session data such as the logged in user, the terminal used, the position the user is currently in an application, and many more. An attacker may attempt to modify the source of the context data to bypass context-based security tools such as these.

Detecting changes to the current database security made by an attacker can be complex because in general security for each database will be different across many vertical channels or individual niche businesses. The security of the database quite obviously depends on what the organization has implemented.

The best way to detect any change to the database security would be to compare the security audit of a known good database with that of the breached database. Commercial scanning tools such as PFCLScan can be easily used to perform such scans. Any differences in the security located between two databases may not be due to an attacker, but may simply be that the security has not been applied consistently in the first place. A difference in the security should be used as a basis to then investigate further. The changes in the security are likely to fall into a number of categories. These include grants to objects, grants of privileges, grants of roles, parameter changes, and setting changes within the database. Once the actual difference is isolated then individual investigations can be made to try to ascertain when the change was made and by who and how. Similar techniques to last section can be used to do this.

Object Changes

Detecting changes to objects in the database such as tables, views, or procedures is slightly better than detecting changes to privileges described earlier in this chapter. This is because the base storage for objects in the database also includes date and timestamp columns. These columns can be used to locate any object that has been added to the database and any changes made to an existing object in the database. This will not include the deletion of an object, as it will no longer exist in the base table.

Deleted objects can again be located by analyzing the system tablespace datafile for deleted records or use of LogMiner can be made to find the changes that deleted an object such as a procedure. A further method can be used to infer deleted objects, which involves looking for missing object IDs or rowids. This could be a simple first step before resorting to mining redo logs or analyzing system tablespace files.

Further evidence may be obtained from audit trails or from the SQL in the SGA. Figure 2-1 shows a detailed data extract from the object table in the data dictionary.

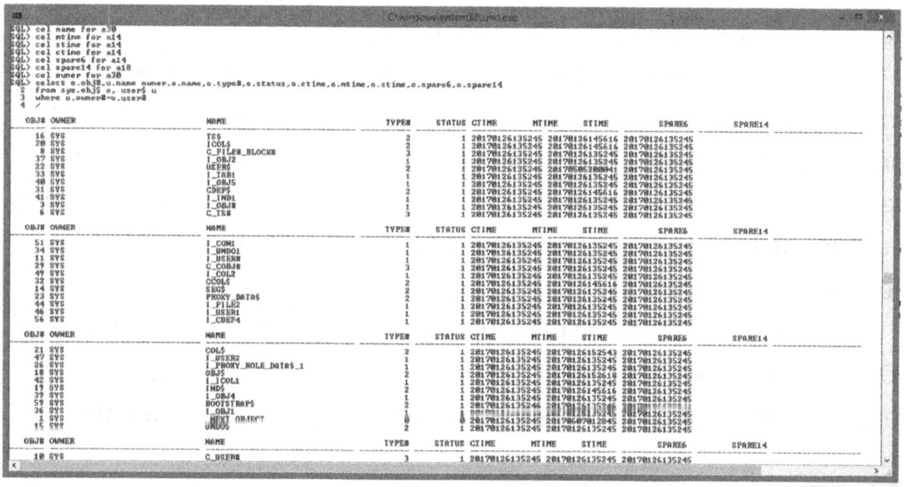

Figure 2-1. *Detailed data extract from the object table in the data dictionary*

There are three main date fields in this table. CTIME is the creation time of the object in the database. STIME is the last load time of the object into the database. MTIME is the last time the object was compiled. When a new object is added to the database such as a PL/SQL procedure then all three-time fields are set. When an object is reloaded to the database, for example by running a script with create or replace in it, then the STIME timestamp is changed because the object is reloaded and the MTIME timestamp is changed because the object is recompiled. If the object is just compiled with the ALTER...COMPILE syntax, then just the MTIME timestamp is changed.

47

Redo Based

Oracle stores redo logs on the database server usually in a multiplexed manner. The redo logs contain a binary representation of all the changes that have been applied to the database during the period of the redo log. The redo log is a fixed size and its space is reused by a circular buffer stored in memory in the SGA. The Oracle database decides when to commit the circular buffer to the redo log for more permanent storage. The redo log itself is not permanent as it is overwritten. The length of time that data will stay in a redo log is dependent on the size of the database, the size of the redo log, and the amount of activity on the database.

If archive logging is enabled, then the redo logs are also periodically written to archive logs. These archive logs contain a complete history of changes to the database since logging began. The archive logs and redo logs' purpose is to enable point-in-time recovery of the database to reapply changes made by end users automatically by use of the binary history in the redo log.

Other tools exist to mine redo logs or to manipulate redo logs. Oracle CDC, Streams, and Goldengate can be used to process redo logs in various ways, primarily in the area of reapplying particular changes to another database.

Oracle also provides a tool called LogMiner, which is a PL/SQL package that allows mining of the redo logs to take place. There are also third-party libraries available on the Internet written in C such as Zizzy that allow redo logs to be mined from C programs.

Mining blocks and redo is time consuming and error prone as it's not consistent in all commands. If the database is large and there is an enormous amount of activity in the timestamp you want to investigate, you must enable the location of the correct archive log redo log in advance.

LogMiner can be used to track any DML or DDL statements executed against the database. Because of the logical way that redo is stored, all of these actions will be in the correct order.

Redo analysis should be a later step, because it is more complex to locate and mine the redo logs than it is to start with simple artifacts from the database servers.

ID Based Searches

An alternative approach to locating deleted data is to use an ID based search. A lot of tables in the Oracle data dictionary and in application tables will invariably have a database column that is some form of ID. Quite often the ID is generated sequentially. One approach to locate deleted data without resorting to log mining or analyzing database datafiles is to first look for gaps in IDs. Listing 2-5 shows a simple example in an Oracle 12.2.0.1 database where a user has been deleted from the database.

Listing 2-5. Examples Locating a Deleted User by Inference

```
SQL> col user# for 999999999999
SQL> col name for a30
SQL> col ctime for a14
SQL> col ptime for a14
SQL> col type for a4
SQL> set lines 220
SQL> select user#,name,decode(type#,0,'ROLE',1,'USER')
type,ctime,ptime
  2  from sys.user$
  3  order by user#
  4  /
```

USER#	NAME	TYPE	CTIME	PTIME
0	SYS	USER	20170126135325	20170429173751
1	PUBLIC	ROLE	20170126135325	
2	CONNECT	ROLE	20170126135325	

...

USER#	NAME	TYPE	CTIME	PTIME
113	PETE7	USER	20170607174845	20170607174845
114	PETE8	USER	20170607174902	20170607174902
116	PETE9	USER	20170607174922	20170607174922
117	_NEXT_USER	ROLE	20170126135325	

...

It is clear from this example that there is a user ID missing from the user$ table. This is ID 115. We can assess when this user was added and deleted by looking at the timestamps of users 114 and 116. Logically, the user that has been deleted must been created after 17:49:02 on 7 June 2017. Determining when it was deleted is harder. Clearly, it was deleted after its creation time and before now. But there is no way to know exactly when it was deleted, because it could have been deleted two seconds after it was created or it could have been deleted two minutes before the review of the table just now.

Further analysis could take place to look for the deleted record in the system tablespace datafile or by using LogMiner.

A further example shown in Figure 2-2 is based on one of the first Oracle forensic pieces work I did approximately 14 years ago. The initial hook into the investigation was to analyze the audit trail listed by date and then listed by rowid. This was done by loading the audit trail from the target system into another local database so that multiple queries could be run against it without changing the audit trail. If the audit trail was ordered by rowid then rowids were missing and some dates were out of sequence. If, on the other hand, the audit trails were ordered by date, then the rowids were out of sequence. The conclusion from this was the records had been deleted from this table and some records have been modified to change their entries and dates. Further analysis using LogMiner confirmed this.

```
Oracle SQL*Plus                                                        _ □ x
File  Edit  Search  Options  Help
SQL> l
  1   select rowid,userid,action#,obj$name
  2* from sys.aud$
SQL> /

ROWID             USERID   ACTION# OBJ$NAME
----------------- -------- ------- --------------------
AAAAIuAABAAABFKAAA SCOTT      101
AAAAIuAABAAABFKAAC X          101
AAAAIuAABAAABFKAAD SYSTEM     100
AAAAIuAABAAABFKAAE SYSTEM     100
AAAAIuAABAAABFKAAF SYSTEM     101
AAAAIuAABAAABFKAAG SYSTEM      43 SYSTEM
AAAAIuAABAAABFKAAH X          101
AAAAIuAABAAABFKAAI SYSTEM     101
AAAAIuAABAAABFKAAJ X          101
AAAAIuAABAAABFKAAK SYSTEM     101
AAAAIuAABAAABFKAAL X          101

ROWID             USERID   ACTION# OBJ$NAME
----------------- -------- ------- --------------------
AAAAIuAABAAABFKAAM SYSTEM     101
AAAAIuAABAAABFKAAN SYSTEM     100
AAAAIuAABAAABFKAAO SYSTEM      43 SYSTEM
AAAAIuAABAAABFKAAP SYSTEM       7 AUD$

15 rows selected.

SQL>
```

Figure 2-2. *A simple example showing detection of deleted data by missing rowid (c) Copyright PeteFinnigan.co Ltd, used with permission*

Applications Data

Similar to looking for missing IDs in user$ presented in the last section, the same approach can be made with application data. Application data often uses sequences when records are generated and added to a table. Similar checks can be made in specific circumstances for missing records. The applications table also often contain other useful data such as audit, user details, and timestamps that can also be used to isolate actions and by whom when an attacker has accessed data in the application.

Some applications, such as the E-Business Suite from Oracle, include specific columns in most tables that record the last user that changed the records in the table and when. They also often include who created the record and when.

51

The specifics of the structure of these tables and usage in forensics is going to be very specific to each investigation. Keep in mind the application tables can often keep track of what users have done throughout the application suite, which could be useful.

Internals

Oracle has limited internal tables that may also be useful for forensic analysis. The three most common ones are discussed here:

- v$db_object_cache: This displays database objects that are cached in the library cache. Different types of records exist in this view. The type of record is distinguished by the namespace column. This includes objects, code, SQL via cursors, and more. Not all of the details in this view survive the database stop and restart, but some do. Even in a busy database, I have seen records from months previous. Figure 2-3 shows sample output from this view.

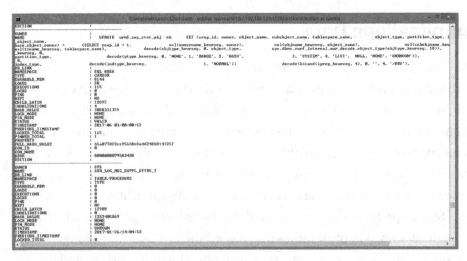

Figure 2-3. *Example output from the library cache. Copyright (c) PeteFinnigan.com Limited. Used with permission.*

- col_usage$: The Oracle optimizer, when a query is
  parsed, decides on the best and most efficient options
  to use when executing the SQL. As part of this process,
  the optimizer stores details of database table columns
  that are accessed in a predicate (a where clause). This
  table can be useful in determining if an attacker has
  accessed a particular table in a select query. A record
  in this table will be transient as Oracle reuses the space.
  An entry will only appear if the query included a where
  clause. Listing 2-6 shows a sample session to create an
  entry in col_usage$. First we extract the object ID for
  the USER$ table and the column ID for the NAME column.
  We then query the USER$ table using a LIKE predicate.
  And finally we query the COL_USAGE$ table to show the
  entry. This information is clearly circumstantial. The
  number of types of predicates that have been used
  against the particular table are just updated. The only
  thing of use is the timestamp to know when the table
  was last accessed. The table such as USER$ is a bad
  example because almost every query in the database
  accesses this table to check permissions. If we were
  trying to find whether a particular application table had
  been accessed, then this would likely yield better results.

Listing 2-6. Queries Visible in col_usage$

```
SQL> select object_id from dba_objects where object_name='USER$';

OBJECT_ID
----------
       22
...
```

```
SQL> col column_id for 999
SQL> col column_name for a30
SQL> l
  1  select column_id, column_name from dba_tab_columns
  2* where table_name='USER$'
SQL> /

COLUMN_ID COLUMN_NAME
--------- ------------------------------
        1 USER#
        2 NAME
        3 TYPE#
        4 PASSWORD
        5 DATATS#
...
SQL> select password from sys.user$ where name like 'SYSTE%';

PASSWORD
----------------------------------------------------------------

SQL>
...
SQL> @print 'select * from col_usage$ where obj#=22 and
intcol#=2'
old  33:          --lv_str:=translate('&&1','''','''''');
new  33:          --lv_str:=translate('select * from col_usage$
                  where obj#=22 and intcol#=2','''','''''');
old  34:          print('&&1');
new  34:          print('select * from col_usage$ where obj#=22
                  and intcol#=2');
Executing Query [select * from col_usage$ where obj#=22 and
intcol#=2]
OBJ#                         : 22
```

```
INTCOL#                         : 2
EQUALITY_PREDS                  : 341
EQUIJOIN_PREDS                  : 83
NONEQUIJOIN_PREDS               : 0
RANGE_PREDS                     : 0
LIKE_PREDS                      : 0
NULL_PREDS                      : 64
TIMESTAMP                       : 20170607183634
FLAGS                           : 16
-------------------------------------------
```

PL/SQL procedure successfully completed.

SQL>

- mon_mods$, mon_mods_all$, dba_tab_modifications,
  all_tab_modifications, and user_tab_moldifications:
  These tables and views record changes that are
  been made to a particular table that was monitored.
  Timestamps as well as statistics are also available in
  these tables. Again, although these views and tables
  will show a very high-level picture as to the last access
  to a particular table (if it is being monitored), they
  will not give the detail of exactly when something
  happened and who did it. It could be a useful starting
  point though.

Flashback and Recycle

Flashback is an extremely useful feature of the database that allows
individual objects or even a complete database to be flashed back in time.
If flashback is enabled, then a flashback query can be used to compare
data in the past with current data. This is useful to look for data or objects

that have changed, added, or deleted recently. You can check if flashback is enabled with the following query:

```
SQL> select flashback_on from v$database;

FLASHBACK_ON
------------------
NO

SQL>
```

The Oracle recycle bin is also useful in forensic analysis. If an attacker dropped an object and he doesn't understand the recycle bin, the object that he dropped may be still in the recycle bin. Checking if the recycle bin is on can be done with this command:

```
SQL> sho parameter recyclebin

NAME                                 TYPE        VALUE
------------------------------------ ----------- --------------
recyclebin                           string      on
SQL>
```

To see the contents of the recycle bin, issue the following command:

```
SQL> show recyclebin
```

The recycle bin carries useful source data of objects that may have been dropped.

Database Audit

The Oracle database provides a number of different audit trail solutions. The core audit solution writes audit records to SYS.AUD$ and must be enabled with an initialization parameter to allow writing to this table. Individual audit commands must then be issued to audit privileges, statements, and object access. The core audit is still available in Oracle 12c but Oracle 12c also now provides a new audit solution called *unified audit*. This is not really completely new, as it still uses the same features as a core audit but now from within policies and a read-only audit trail. If unified audit is enabled in pure mode, then core auditing no longer works. Core auditing also supports writing the audit trail to the operating system as text files or XML and the possibility to syslog.

There are other audit trail opportunities within the database, including the audit of superuser privileges to trace files on the operating system and fine-grained auditing in the enterprise edition of Oracle. Some of the other components installed in the Oracle database (usually cost options), including database vault, have their own audit trail. Some of the components such as RMAN and can generate their own audit. Other tools, such as BI, also have their own audit trails. Oracle's product E-Business Suite also has comprehensive auditing built in. Products such as E-Business Suite allow row-level auditing using triggers.

Customers have often developed and built their own audit trail solutions, sometimes using Oracle features and sometimes using triggers. There is also a possibility to use system triggers to audit almost 50 different actions in a 12c database, including logon, log off, start-up, shutdown, DDL, errors, and much more.

It is possible to correlate across most audit trails and the database sessions. Oracle maintains a common ID for audit records that can be linked to the session ID and the ID used in fine-grained auditing. The only flaw with this is that there does not seem to be a way to link unified audit with the traditional core audit. This can be solved quite easily with use of a logon trigger that stores the link between the two.

If auditing is enabled in the database, that is to be investigated. The first step is to understand all of the audit settings that have been enabled for core audit, unified audit, application audit, fine-grained audit, and more. Once the range of audit settings is known, the trails can be targeted and used in the investigation.

Database Dumps

Oracle allows almost every component of its structure to be dumped to trace file. This includes many areas of the SGA, datafiles, redo logs, control files, and much more. Oracle has very comprehensive instrumentation that allows many elements of its functionality to be traced and generate trace files. Even the complete SGA can be dumped to a text file for later analysis, which can be useful for forensics. Individual areas of the SGA, such as the library cache, can be dumped separately. Listing 2-7 shows how to dump the library cache to the trace file.

Listing 2-7. Dumping the Library Cache to Show a Password Change

```
SQL> alter session set events 'immediate trace name library_
cache level 10';

Session altered

SQL>
```

Figure 2-4 shows the results of this dump command. Internal details of the library cache are revealed as well as the actual DDL that was issued to change the system password.

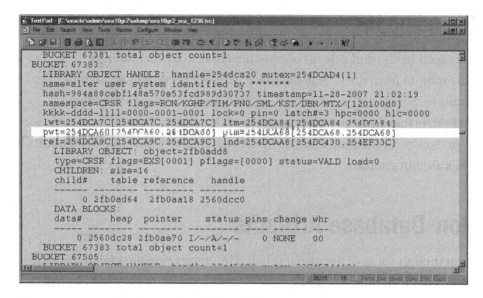

Figure 2-4. *A library cache dump (c) Copyright PeteFinnigan.com Limited. Used with permission.*

Oracle has many interfaces to allow trace to be set. This includes packages such as DBMS_SYSTEM, DBMS_MONITOR, the oradebug tool, and various ALTER SYSTEM and ALTER SESSION commands. Dumping something from a compromised database should be considered carefully. Dumping the SGA will generate an enormous text file and impact the SGA slightly. There are no standard tools available to review trace files or dumps that have been created. There are trace files analyzer tools for standard SQL trace but these are not useful for forensics unless the attacker accessed with some SQL trace enabled.

Consider all the different possibilities of dumping, particularly the ability to dump specific data blocks from a file. The one flaw with this is that the standard trace file does not include the deleted data.

Rounding Up

This section showed a flavor of possible areas to extract forensic information from the Oracle database. Explore these and all of their nuances. For instance, for extracting SQL, there are over 100 tables and views that can potentially hold SQL statements. There is a massive opportunity for locating forensic data in an Oracle database even if audit trails are not enabled.

Non-Database Artifacts

Even though some of the artifacts listed in this section are effectively part of the Oracle database, they fit better in this section, as they are not true database artifacts since they are not actually in the database. Any forensic investigation of an Oracle database should not just focus on the database. The database does not run in isolation; it runs on a Windows server or a Unix type server in general. Therefore, there are database artifacts that can be collected from the file system of the operating system, such as the logs from the database and logs and other information from the server.

This section discusses some of these artifacts and how they might be useful during forensic analysis.

Webserver Logs

The logs that are available depend on the actual web server that is being used. There can also be application server logs that may prove useful. In general, a web-based application will receive data from an end user through a web form and an application server will convert this into a SQL statements that are sent to the database. Sometimes there is a separate application server that does this work and sometimes it's a plugin to the web server.

Most web servers, such as Apache or IIS, have very similar log file formats. There is usually an access log and an error log. We are interested in the error log particularly during the time scale of the attack because if an attacker is attempting to connect to the database via something like SQL injection, then it's likely the errors are going to be generated and some of those will end up in the error log for the web server. If the attacker succeeds in connecting to the database via the web site then there can also be entries in the access log that are attributable to the attacker. That's why we're very interested in the access log as well.

Web server logs follow a standard format so it's easy to understand and deal with. Some tools are available to parse web server logs but generally these are related to web site statistics and access patterns. Some of the major log repository software such as Splunk support transfer storage and reporting on web server logs. Listing 2-8 shows a small amount of output from a typical Apache error log. This output may or may not be attributed to an attack. There is very little to go on.

Listing 2-8. Typical Output from an Apache Error Log

```
[root@oel59orablog logs]# tail -f error log
 [Fri Jun 02 23:55:19 2017] [error] [client 192.168.1.56] File
does not exist: /usr/local/apache2/htdocs/favicon.ico
[Sat Jun 03 00:10:33 2017] [error] [client 192.168.1.56] File
does not exist: /usr/local/apache2/htdocs/favicon.ico
[Sat Jun 03 00:18:32 2017] [error] [client 192.168.1.56] File
does not exist: /usr/local/apache2/htdocs/browserconfig.xml
[Sat Jun 03 00:23:50 2017] [error] [client 192.168.1.56] File
does not exist: /usr/local/apache2/htdocs/browserconfig.xml
```

Listing 2-9 shows a sample of output from an Apache access log. In this case, the output is very telling as it shows probable SQL injection against the database that supports the web site.

Listing 2-9. Sample Apache Access Log Showing SQL Injection

```
[root@oel59orablog logs]# tail -f access_log
192.168.1.56 - - [03/Jun/2017:01:54:16 +0100] "GET /index.php?s
=x%25%27%29%29%29%29a%29%2F**%2Funion%2F**%2Fselect%2F**%2F33%2
C1%2Cto_timestamp%28%2727-OCT-13%27%29%2Cto_timestamp%28%2727-
OCT-13%27%29%2Ctable_name%2C%27x%27%2C0%2Cnull%2C%27publish%27
%2C%27open%27%2C%27open%27%2Cnull%2C%27name%27%2Cnull%2Cnull%2
Cto_timestamp%28%2727-OCT-13%27%29%2Cto_timestamp%28%2727-OCT-
13%27%29%2Cnull%2C0%2Cnull%2C0%2Cnull%2Cnull%2C0%2C6%2F**%2Ffro
m%2F**%2Fuser_tables-- HTTP/1.1" 200 17549
192.168.1.56 - - [03/Jun/2017:01:54:38 +0100] "GET /wp-login.
php HTTP/1.1" 200 1464
192.168.1.56 - - [03/Jun/2017:01:54:44 +0100] "POST /wp-login.
php HTTP/1.1" 200 1806
192.168.1.56 - - [03/Jun/2017:01:56:19 +0100] "GET /index.php?s
=x%25%27%29%29%29%29a%29%2F**%2Funion%2F**%2Fselect%2F**%2F33%2
C1%2Cto_timestamp%28%2727-OCT-13%27%29%2Cto_timestamp%28%2727-
OCT-13%27%29%2C%27CardNumber-%27%7C%7Cname_on_card%7C%7C%27-
%27%7C%7Cbof_kkrc.dr%28cc34%29%2C%27x%27%2C0%2Cnull%2C%27publis
h%27%2C%27open%27%2C%27open%27%2Cnull%2C%27name%27%2Cnull%2Cnu
ll%2Cto_timestamp%28%2727-OCT-13%27%29%2Cto_timestamp%28%2727-
OCT-13%27%29%2Cnull%2C0%2Cnull%2C0%2Cnull%2Cnull%2C0%2C6%2F**%2
Ffrom%2F**%2Forablog.bof_pay_details-- HTTP/1.1" 200 5367
```

SQL Injection attempts in this logger are very clear because of the
PL/SQL comment visible at the end of the URL. Also the URL does not look
like the earlier entries where someone has attempted to get to the login
page; they are very simple and clean URLs. The other URLs are clearly SQL.

Application Logs

If the application runs on a server, then be sure to access the logs that relate to the application. These can prove useful in the analysis. The exact location of these logs and their format and the contents are unknown in advance. If the application runs locally on a PC, then tho logs can be requested for the application but only for the PC that indicates where the attack came from. This requires further investigation to try to establish where the attacker is located and if the attacker is using an application that you have access to.

If the attack is remote and not an employee of the company, then this is not possible. Applications often generate external files such text-based or binary-based reports and sometimes there are data dumps written to the operating system of the application server. If necessary, request any files created during the time period of the attack from the application server.

Operating System Audit

Most modern operating systems support audit trails. This is true of Windows, Linux, and Solaris. As part of the analysis, establish if auditing is enabled on the server. If auditing is enabled then request the audit logs from the server. These can be used to correlate with the time period of the attack to assess if the attacker was able to access the operating system from the database. If the attacker actually gained access to the database from the operating system in the first place, then these logs are also important. Different operating systems support completely different types of audit trails; therefore, establish which operating system is supporting the database and the possible audit solutions that may be present.

On a Linux operating system also request or obtain all the messages for security, log in, etc. Also on a Unix operating system, request or obtain the history files from every user's shell account. This will give you an indication as to whether anyone accessed the database directly or another database on another server from the breached server. Again this may give you an indication if the attacker was able to access the operating system from the database.

TNS Listener Logs

The database listener may be set up to run on the database server or it could be on a remote server, particularly when RAC is used and enabled. In fact, there may be multiple listeners in a RAC environment. For each database listener, establish the location of the log file. This can be found from the listener.ora file and by using a status command within the listener. A sample status command is shown in Listing 2-10.

Listing 2-10. A Sample Listener Status Command

```
LSNRCTL> status
Connecting to (DESCRIPTION=(ADDRESS=(PROTOCOL=TCP)(HOST=oel7.
localdomain)(PORT=1539)))
STATUS of the LISTENER
------------------------
Alias                    LISTENER
Version                  TNSLSNR for Linux: Version
                         12.2.0.1.0 - Production
Start Date               02-JUN-2017 10:39:51
Uptime                   5 days 10 hr. 8 min. 55 sec
Trace Level              off
Security                 ON: Local OS Authentication
SNMP                     OFF
Listener Parameter File  /u01/app/oracle/product/12.2.0/
                         dbhome_1/network/admin/listener.ora
Listener Log File        /u01/app/oracle/diag/tnslsnr/oel7/
                         listener/alert/log.xml
```

```
Listening Endpoints Summary...
  (DESCRIPTION=(ADDRESS=(PROTOCOL=tcp)(HOST=oel7.localdomain)
(PORT=1539)))
  (DESCRIPTION=(ADDRESS=(PROTOCOL=ipc)(KEY=EXTPROC1521)))
  (DESCRIPTION=(ADDRESS=(PROTOCOL=tcps)(HOST=oel7.localdomain)
(PORT=5500))(Security=(my_wallet_directory=/u01/app/oracle/
admin/orcl/xdb_wallet))(Presentation=HTTP)(Session=RAW))
Services Summary...
Service "orcl.localdomain" has 1 instance(s).
  Instance "orcl", status READY, has 1 handler(s) for this
service...
Service "orclXDB.localdomain" has 1 instance(s).
  Instance "orcl", status READY, has 1 handler(s) for this
service...
The command completed successfully
```

The log file location is visible in the header of the status command. This log file can then be located on the operating system and its contents can be used as part of a forensic investigation. The log file shows details of every connection to the database. The log file can be summarized to establish high-level counts of connections from the IP address, the terminal, users, and more. The listener log file is the only place where the full path to the program used to make the connection to the database is visible. Listing 2-11 shows a sample entry from an Oracle 12.2.0.1 listener log file.

Listing 2-11. Sample Contents of a Listener Log File

```
...
<msg time='2017-06-07T19:05:41.460+01:00' org_id='oracle'
comp_id='tnslsnr'
 type='UNKNOWN' level='16' host_id='oel7.localdomain'
 host_addr='192.168.1.95' pid='2991'>
```

```
<txt>07-JUN-2017 19:05:41 * (CONNECT_DATA=(SERVICE_NAME=orcl.
localdomain)(CID=(PROGRAM=C:\_aa\PB\bin\sqlplus.exe)
(HOST=HACKER-DEV)(USER=Pete))) * (ADDRESS=(PROTOCOL=tcp)
(HOST=192.168.1.56)(PORT=62829)) * establish * orcl.localdomain
* 0
 </txt>
</msg>
...
```

Arup Nanda wrote a great three-part paper on mining information from the Oracle listener log. This is available from http://www.dbazine. com/oracle/or-articles/nanda14.

SQL*Net Trace

SQL*Net log files and trace files can be generated on the database server or client PCs. These are unlikely to relate to an attack unless the DBA has enabled SQL*Net logging automatically on the server. Any log file generated on the client PC can be accessed but doesn't provide much value. SQL*Net trace, if set to level 16 or support level, will include network packet contents.

For completeness, search the server for any log or trace files and check if they occur during the period of the attack. However, it is unlikely the hacker would generate logs files for his own activities.

SYSDBA Audit Trace Files and Logs

There are three levels of audit within the traditional Oracle database audit system. The first is the audit trail that is generated by settings enabled in the database, where this audit trail is written to the database, to operating system files, or to syslog. The second is SYSDBA auditing, which is enabled when the initialization parameter audit_sys_operations=true. If this is enabled, then all top-level actions as SYSDBA and SYSOPER are logged to trace files that are located on the server and pointed out by the initialization parameter audit_file_dest. Finally, there is mandatory audit. This is the audit that generated when anyone makes a connection as SYSDBA or SYSOPER. This audit also captures startup, shutdown, and basic recovery details. The mandatory audit cannot be disabled. The previous two audits for SYSDBA and standard database auditing can of course be disabled.

The mandatory audit and the SYSDBA audit when written to trace files causes a lot of files to be created. Each process that is running in the database has a separate PID and each process generates its own audit trace file. If a process starts and there is already an audit trace file for the same PID, then the new audit records are appended to that same file. If a process starts and there is no trace file for the PID then a new file is created and the audit records are written to. This can quickly generate thousands of audit trace files, which become difficult to manage and difficult to analyze. There are no standard tools to aid in this process. There is a view in the database called V$XML_AUDIT_TRAIL that allows these trace files to be viewed with SQL, but only if SYSDBA auditing is enabled and the audit trail is set to be generated as XML. There are also a lot of bugs in this functionality, making it unreliable.

Simple grep commands can be used to analyze these trace files. These can be used to locate all the different database users, operating system users, terminals, programs, and actions that have been used against the database. Of course, some of these include SQL. The audit settings can be seen in Listing 2-12.

Listing 2-12. The Audit Trail Settings in the Database

```
SQL> show parameter aud

NAME                     TYPE      VALUE                          ,
--------------------     --------  ------------------------------
audit_file_dest          string    /u01/app/oracle/admin/orcl/
                                   adump
audit_sys_operations     boolean   TRUE
audit_syslog_level       string
audit_trail              string    DB
```

There are currently 426 such trace files on my Oracle 12.2.0.1 database server:

```
[oracle@oel7 adump]$ ls -al | wc -l
426
[oracle@oel7 adump]$
```

Sample contents of one trace file are shown in Listing 2-13. Trace file includes high-level information such as the database version of the operating system platform, but very little to allow correlation with other forensic sources. The two values that are of use are the Unix PID and the Oracle process number, as these can be matched to values in the database session.

Listing 2-13. Sample SYSDBA Trace File

```
Audit file /u01/app/oracle/admin/orcl/adump/orcl_ora_8628_20170
604192652037318143795.aud
Oracle Database 12c Standard Edition Release 12.2.0.1.0 - 64bit
Production
Build label:    RDBMS_12.2.0.1.0_LINUX.X64_170125
ORACLE_HOME:    /u01/app/oracle/product/12.2.0/dbhome_1
System name:    Linux
```

```
Node name:        oel7.localdomain
Release:          3.8.13-118.17.5.el7uek.x86_64
Version:          #2 SMP Wed Apr 12 09:11:03 PDT 2017
Machine:          x86_64
Instance name: orcl
Redo thread mounted by this instance: 1
Oracle process number: 26
Unix process pid: 8628, image: oracle@oel7.localdomain
...
Sun Jun  4 19:27:13 2017 +01:00
LENGTH : '357'
ACTION :[33] 'select count(*) from v$sql_cursor'
DATABASE USER:[3] 'SYS'
PRIVILEGE :[6] 'SYSDBA'
CLIENT USER:[4] 'Pete'
CLIENT TERMINAL:[10] 'HACKER-DEV'
STATUS:[1] '0'
DBID:[10] '1470381799'
SESSIONID:[10] '4294967295'
USERHOST:[20] 'WORKGROUP\HACKER-DEV'
CLIENT ADDRESS:[54] '(ADDRESS=(PROTOCOL=tcp)(HOST=192.168.1.56)
(PORT=2656))'
ACTION NUMBER:[1] '3'
```

Database Trace

Oracle can generate many different types of trace files. These include
trace files generated by core dumps, trace files generated by background
processes, and trace files generated by end users. Listing 2-14 shows how
to find these trace files.

Listing 2-14. How to Find Trace Files

```
SQL> sho parameter dump_dest
```

```
NAME                     TYPE     VALUE
------------------------  -------  -------------------------------
background_dump_dest      string   /u01/app/oracle/product/12.2.0/
                                   dbhome_1/rdbms/log
core_dump_dest            string   /u01/app/oracle/diag/rdbms/orcl/
                                   orcl/cdump
user_dump_dest            string   /u01/app/oracle/product/12.2.0/
                                   dbhome_1/rdbms/log
```

```
SQL>
```

Trace files can contain a lot of useful information for forensic analysis. Initial analysis should focus on directory listings, including the timestamps of the files. Target the trace files that match the date range of the attack. Inspect the trace files for evidence of the attacker. If an attacker causes an error in the database, then it could cause a core dump, which could generate trace file. Trace files can include SQL and memory of the stack or the heap of the Oracle process that was running when the error occurred. Then this may give details of what the attacker was doing. Each trace file includes SID and serial, which can be used to cross-reference with other artifacts from the database. It's unlikely that an attacker would generate a user-level trace during his attack, but it's possible. If some hacker was attempting to understand how something worked, then he may do this, so don't discount user trace.

Database Datafiles

The database is made up of many files, including the datafiles that hold the actual database. Listing 2-15 shows how to find the locations of these datafiles. The default permissions on the datafiles should be secure. Accessing the datafiles directly with commands such as strings on Unix allows you to see data easily. Character data is stored in clear text normally, numbers are obfuscated with a simple scheme, and dates are stored in a Julian format.

Listing 2-15. Locating the Datafiles

```
SQL> col file_id for 99
SQL> col file_name for a40
SQL> col tablespace_name for a20
SQL> set lines 120
SQL> select file_id,file_name,tablespace_name
  2  from dba_data_files;

FILE_ID FILE_NAME                                     TABLESPACE_NAME
------- ---------------------------------------- ------- -----------
      1 /u01/app/oracle/oradata/orcl/system01.dbf  SYSTEM
      3 /u01/app/oracle/oradata/orcl/sysaux01.dbf  SYSAUX
      7 /u01/app/oracle/oradata/orcl/users01.dbt   USERS
      4 /u01/app/oracle/oradata/orcl/undotbs01.dbf UNDOTBS1

SQL> select file_id,file_name,tablespace_name
  2  from dba_temp_files;

FILE_ID FILE_NAME                                     TABLESPACE_NAME
------- -------------------------------------------- ------------
      1 /u01/app/oracle/oradata/orcl/temp01.dbf    TEMP
```

If necessary, the system tablespace datafile can be copied, checksummed, and then used for analysis to locate deleted data.

The online redo logs can be located with the SQL in Listing 2-16.

Listing 2-16. Location of the Redo Logs

```
SQL> col type for a6
SQL> col member for a50
SQL> select type,member from v$logfile;

TYPE    MEMBER
------  --------------------------------------------------
ONLINE /u01/app/oracle/oradata/orcl/redo03.log
ONLINE /u01/app/oracle/oradata/orcl/redo02.log
ONLINE /u01/app/oracle/oradata/orcl/redo01.log

SQL>
```

The archive logs can be located using the V$ARCHIVED_LOG view and this command:

```
SQL> archive log list
Database log mode              No Archive Mode
Automatic archival             Disabled
Archive destination            /u01/app/oracle/product/12.2.0/
                               dbhome_1/dbs/arch
Oldest online log sequence     8
Current log sequence           10
SQL>
```

Rounding Up

The database includes many external artifacts such as database datafiles, redo logs, and archive logs. There are also other files of interest, such as the password file. The initialization parameter file (`init.ora` and `spfile.ora`). The database also has a central log file called the alert log, which includes information about database shutdown and restart, structural changes to the database, and database errors. The alert log is worth including in the forensic analysis, particularly for the errors.

The biggest gap in the analysis process is the lack of availability of free standard tools to analyze the trace files and log files oracle produces. These can still be viewed by hand of course using simple tools such as `grep`.

Correlation

Correlation can help immensely during a forensic analysis. If you can locate one piece of information that is relevant to the investigation, then because of the complex structure of Oracle, it's more than likely that another piece of information can also be located and correlated with the first. There are many fields that can be correlated. Figure 2-5 shows the contents of an Excel spreadsheet that was created to compare columns of data from the Oracle session information, `SYS_CONTEXT` information, database trigger attributes, and the core Oracle database audit trail.

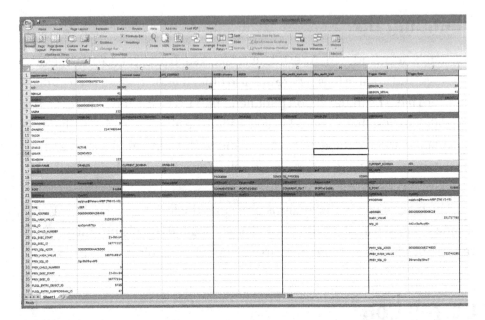

Figure 2-5. *A study of correlated columns Copyright (c) 2017, PeteFinnigan.com Limited. Used with permission.*

This spreadsheet contains by no means all possible fields that could be correlated, in fact around 185 different fields. Even so, there is still not a great deal of correlation between just these four areas. In fact, there are only six fields that correlate across all four areas of session, context, trigger, and audit (actually we compare AUD$ and DBA_AUDIT_TRAIL so there are actually five areas). Even among the six fields, Oracle is not good at naming conventions. For instance, the operating system user field is called OSUSER, OS_USER, SPARE4, and OS_USERNAME. There is also confusion with some fields where the column name does match but the data is different such as the process number.

In general, we can correlate two main things—the first is time and the second is any number of other fields such as session ID, operating system user, database username, and many more. In the case of time correlation, it may be that there is no other field that can be matched but if something was changed in the database at around the exact same time then it could be significant, but only if we can match records. The fact that only six fields can be matched out of 185 is not actually a big problem because with the six fields we can match across each of these areas and gain additional columns of data.

If you don't know what to search for   i.c. you have been hacked but not sure how—but know you the time period, then you can use the timestamp to locate all evidence and correlate it with other data.

Many other views and tables in the database can also be correlated to these five core areas, which enables artifacts that you gather to be matched to each other. Some of the areas that you can correlate with include trace files; these can be matched on time stamps and the SID and serial included in every trace file. You can also match on user IDs or object IDs or any other data just as you can with any business relational logic; the same applies with forensics. If it's possible to match records, then they can be added to the analysis.

Correlation can take place with external sources such as the trace files just mentioned, SQL*Net log files, listener log files, web server logs, operating system logs, and more. In these cases, it is still possible to match with data in the database such as timestamps, users, process IDs, and more.

Correlation is a powerful tool that can be used as part of the analysis.

Deleted Data

In traditional forensic analysis of a desktop PC, the target machine would be taken away by law enforcement and the hard disk copied for forensic analysis. Some of the high-level processes involved in this were discussed earlier in the chain of custody section in Chapter 1. In this process it is important that the copy of the hard disk is an exact byte-for-byte copy. This is verified by performing a checksum of the original disc and a copy. Starting the target machine would likely change the hard disk, as any

PC operating system would generate logs or modify static files as part of its startup and shutdown process. Therefore, techniques for analyzing a target machine usually involve mounting the disc in read-only mode, often with byte blocker software or even hardware to ensure that the disc is not changed and only read. In general, the analysis of a read-only hard disk would involve looking for certain types of documents—text files or images perhaps—and documenting those. It may also involve looking for deleted files or data where the perpetrator has tried to hide their actions. Forensic investigators of PCs are often equipped with software or even hardware such as an electron microscope in rare cases when deleted data can be recovered. At a simpler level, the PC's recycle bin can be used to find deleted files and simple software can search hard disk for files that have been deleted.

Taking the same analogy to the forensic analysis of an Oracle database is much harder. We could take the same approach with an Oracle database in that we could copy all of the discs involved in the database and then mount them all in a read-only mode and allow only read-only searching of the disc to look for evidence of the attack. This would be much harder to do because there is no off-the-shelf software that would allow the disc to be used as a database in read-only mode. A read-only database in the context of disaster recovery is not what we mean by read-only here. A read-only database still has transient data in the SGA and is still modifying and updating its dictionary. Another concern with copying a database is a size. It is not uncommon to have databases in the many terabytes or even hundreds of terabytes size. It would be expensive to copy every disc from a production database; this method is probably impractical in most cases. The biggest concern with static disk analysis is the lack of the ability to use the database itself to query the data using SQL.

One thing that could still be done is to search the discs for deleted data; in this case data that has been deleted that is part of the actual database. In other words, rows in a database table that have been deleted. Again there is no off-the-shelf software to do this but various people over the years have been involved with writing software that does some of this. At a simplistic level, Oracle sets a single bit in each record to indicate that it is deleted. This allows the database engine to reuse that space when it needs to. In reality in datafiles there is often a lot of deleted data. In some cases, updates to records also involve the deletion of the existing record and the insertion of a new record. So even updated data may look like deleted data.

A number of companies and individuals have written software that allows a crashed database to be recovered. In this case, the intention is not forensic analysis but the recovery of a broken database. The tool from Oracle was called DUL (data unloader). A number of individuals, including Kurt Van Meerbeeck (jDUL/Dude), have written tools to do exactly the same. These tools parsed the datafiles looking for records including deleted data.

A number of years ago David Litchfield wrote some simple tools for parsing datafiles and redo logs in the search for deleted data. David introduced the idea of looking for deleted data in data blocks as well as other Oracle forensics techniques in his seven-part Oracle forensics series—see Chapter 6 for a link that references these papers. David's tools were available on his web site but this is no longer the case. There is no public access to the Litchfield tools any longer and they were not production quality anyway. They were written for much older versions of Oracle (10g). Writing tools such as this to search datafiles for deleted data would be a complex task and involves reverse engineering the datafile format and the redo log format. Any author would need to take into account Oracle running on different operating systems, different endian file systems, and other factors. Although the data block format could change between major versions or even minor patches, this is unlikely. The file format for the Oracle database remains pretty stable over many years. The fact remains that most of the block structure is not documented by Oracle but enough information is available on the Internet to various internal web sites and David's seven-part series on forensics that it would not be impossible to create such tools. So, this was a good idea at the time, but these are not practical reliable tools to be used as part of forensic analysis unless a commercial company invests a lot of time and effort to create production quality tools.

If a PL/SQL procedure was added to the database by an attacker, perhaps used to escalate his rights within the database as part of an SQL Injection and then removed because the attacker wanted to hide, he might think he could get away with it. In reality, because of the complexity of Oracle and the fact that everything related to the structure of the database including code is stored in the data dictionary, it's possible to reconstruct what has been created and then removed. There are a number of techniques that look for deleted objects without using reverse engineering or writing complex tools.

One method is to use LogMiner or direct redo log analysis. LogMiner allows redo logs or archive logs to be mined to locate changes that have occurred in the database. The redo logs store a binary version of all of the changes that have occurred. This is so they can be replayed in a recovery scenario. Although LogMiner can be used to analyze redo logs, it is also possible to dump the redo logs to text-based trace files using `ALTER SYSTEM` commands. The output can be readable text or binary. Unfortunately, the block dump method does not include deleted data. Oracle has provided a number of tools over the years for processing of redo logs, including CDC, Streams, and GoldenGate. The earlier of the tools of now been deprecated in the latter tools are now cost options. So the use of the tools from Oracle to analyze redo are effectively not supported or need additional licenses.

There is a LGPL library (in C) to read Redo logs on sourceforce— `http://www.zizzy.org` and `https://sourceforge.net/projects/zizzy/`. This has not been touched for at least ten years. Use of this library would again be complex and would require skill in the C programming language and detailed knowledge of Oracle. Again, this is not a practical solution for forensic analysis of deleted data.

Remember that the deleted data is transient and could disappear any time. There is no predictable way to understand when a deleted record may be lost. Oracle's internal algorithms decide on whether space should be reused or not. In reality, deleted data will most likely stay in the database for quite some time. Listing 2-17 shows the creation of a procedure, in this case by an attacker. The creation of procedure involves a lot of changes to the database and storage of many artifacts in the data dictionary. A true picture of what happens when procedures are created can be obtained quite easily by running a trace during the creation process. Of course, the hacker would not have run trace; I included this here simply to illustrate what goes on when a procedure is added to the database.

Listing 2-17. Create a Hacker Backdoor Procedure

```
SQL> alter session set sql_trace=true;

Session altered.

SQL> create procedure hacker_backdoor (p in varchar2) as
  2   begin
  3   execute immediate p;
  4   end;
  5   /

Procedure created.

SQL> alter session set sql_trace=false;

Session altered.

SQL>
```

Listing 2-18 shows how many actions have taken place in the database simply by creating a procedure. Even this high-level view of the actions is not a complete list of everything that happens in the database when a procedure is created. A review of these 58 parse statements shows insert, update, delete, and select statements against many dictionary tables and views, including OBJ$, IDL_CHAR$, ACCESS$, DEPENDENCY$, CCOL$, AUDIT$, PROCEDUREPLSQL$, ARGUMENT$, PROCEDUREINFO$, WARNING_SETTINGS$, SETTINGS$, PLSCOPE_SQL$, PLSCOPE_STATEMENT$, PLSCOPE_IDENTIFIERS$, PLSCOPE_ACTION$, OBJAUTH$, SOURCE$, IDL_SB4$, IDL_UB1$, IDL_UB2$, and more. A number of triggers are also executed around the spatial functionality and the PL/SQL itself is compiled. This involves compilation, optimization of the SQL (if there was SQL involved), optimization of PL/SQL, and insertion of the SQL code into the SGA. Hashes of the SQL code are taken and stored as well. This gives a good overview of how complex Oracle is as a database. Anything that occurs in the database that involves changes to the database—i.e., adding a procedure or a user—will involve a large number of actions both in the SGA and against and into the data dictionary. This is good news for forensic analysts, because all of these actions leave traces.

Listing 2-18. Grep of the Trace File to See How Many Actions Take Place When Adding a Procedure to the Database

```
[root@oel7 trace]# grep PARSING orcl_ora_28998.trc | wc -l
58
[root@oel7 trace]#
```

Of course, once the procedure has been compiled, many of the artifacts are created and are visible in the data dictionary. Listing 2-19 shows an example of the procedure details.

Listing 2-19. Details of the Hacker Procedure in the
DBA_PROCEDURES View

```
SQL> select owner,object_name,procedure_name,object_id,object_type
  2  from dba_procedures where object_name='HACKER_BACKDOOR';

OWNER
------------------------------------------------------------------
OBJECT_NAME
------------------------------------------------------------------
PROCEDURE_NAME
------------------------------------------------------------------
 OBJECT_ID OBJECT_TYPE
---------- -------------
SYSTEM
HACKER_BACKDOOR

     75774 PROCEDURE

SQL>
```

The hacker wants to protect his identity and avoid being caught, so
after he does whatever nefarious acts, he deletes his backdoor procedure.
Listing 2-20 shows the deletion of the hacker's procedure.

Listing 2-20. Deletion of the Hacker's Procedure

```
SQL> drop procedure hacker_backdoor;

Procedure dropped.

SQL>
```

Of course, the hacker again will not run a trace on this deletion but
you can expect without any detailed analysis that most of the actions
performed in the compilation of the procedure have to be reversed. This

means removing the entry that includes the source code from SOURCE$, the details of the object from OBJ$, details of the procedure, and its arguments from PROCEDURE$ and ARGUMENT$ and all of the compiled code from the IDL_% tables. Of course, this is just a sample of what it does.

Can we still see the procedure in the database without resorting to reverse engineering tools such as those created by David Litchfield after it has been deleted? Listing 2-21 shows that simple tools can be used to locate strings within the undo tablespace datafile. In this example, I already knew the name of the procedure that I was looking for, so finding it was easy. In a real investigation, the complete contents of the undo tablespace must be reviewed and any procedure or PL/SQL can be extracted and compared with the current database. Of course, the source code of any procedure can also be reviewed to see if it looks nefarious.

Listing 2-21. The Deleted Procedure Visible in the Undo Tablespace Datafile

```
...
[root@oel7 orcl]# strings undotbs01.dbf > /tmp/undo.txt
...
!B]A
!B]W
"HACKER_BACKDOOR"067678E6F74C6F524BBF5F319F6D326C"P"VARCHAR2"SY
S"SYS_STUB_FOR_PURITY_ANALYSIS"PRDS"PWDS"PRPS"PWPS"DE0D653FCD4C
FAD500FF0FC43D33DE57"74E3E828BDE795AC1DD1B0C2F001DD9B"68FEB09BE
098A75F4580EB0A64161B19"E47FC731D0007CFC1F21B274314A5C63"494259
841A7F614198485ACBCC50749D""
end;
execute immediate p;
/ArN
```

```
begin
procedure hacker_backdoor (p in varchar2) as
:K-------------------------------------
rNxu
```

Can the deleted procedure also be viewed in the datafile itself? Without resorting to tools to search datafiles looking for deleted row entries, this is harder to do. This is simply because we would need to find the deleted entries, which would require stepping through data blocks and looking for row entries and then looking for entries that have the deleted flag set. But, we can use simple tools such as Unix strings or open the datafile in a hex editor to search through it to look for things that may be suspicious.

Figure 2-6 shows the system tablespace from the same Oracle version 12.2.0.1 database opened in a hex editor. The HACKER_BACKDOOR procedure was deleted from this database, but as you can see the source code for the procedure is still visible in the datafile. Again this was made simpler because we knew the name of the procedure we were looking for. But, a simple search for source code in the system tablespace datafile can be made by looking for the keywords procedure, function, package, and type and manually searching for the start of the procedure, function, or package source code, as this will indicate that we are most likely in the SOURCE$ records. In the line above the start of the procedure source code we can see 3C; this indicates a deleted record. A non-deleted record would show 2C. The values after 3C indicate the number of columns and column data.

```
31627910:  00 00 00 00 00 00 00 00   00 00 00 00 00 00 00 00   ................
31627920:  00 00 00 00 00 00 00 00   00 00 00 00 00 00 00 00   ................
31627930:  00 00 00 00 00 00 3C 01 03   04 C3 08 3A 4B 02 C1 02   .....<...Ã.:K.Á.
31627940:  2D 70 72 6F 63 65 64 75   72 65 20 68 61 63 6B 65   -procedure hacke
31627950:  72 5F 62 61 63 6B 64 6F   6F 72 20 28 70 20 69 6E   r_backdoor (p in
31627960:  20 76 61 72 63 68 61 72   32 29 20 61 73 0A 3C 01    varchar2) as.<.
31627970:  03 04 C3 08 3A 4B 02 C1   03 06 62 65 67 69 6E 0A   ..Ã.:K.Á..begin.
31627980:  3C 01 03 04 C3 08 3A 4B   02 C1 04 15 65 78 65 63   <...Ã.:K.Á..exec
31627990:  75 74 65 20 69 6D 6D 65   64 69 61 74 65 20 70 3B   ute immediate p;
316279A0:  0A 3C 01 03 04 C3 08 3A   4B 02 C1 05 04 65 6E 64   .<...Ã.:K.Á..end
316279B0:  3B 3C 01 03 04 C3 08 20   35 02 C1 02 2B 46 55 4E   ;<...Ã. 5.Á.+FUN
316279C0:  43 54 49 4F 4E 20 6C 6F   63 61 6C 5F 65 6E 71 75   CTION local_enqu
316279D0:  6F 74 65 5F 6E 61 6D 65   20 28 73 74 72 20 76 61   ote_name (str va
316279E0:  72 63 68 61 72 32 29 0A   3C 01 03 04 C3 08 20 35   rchar2).<...Ã. 5
316279F0:  02 C1 03 14 20 72 65 74   75 72 6E 20 76 61 72 63   .Á.. return varc
31627A00:  68 61 72 32 20 69 73 0A   3C 01 03 04 C3 08 20 35   har2 is.<...Ã. 5
31627A10:  02 C1 04 09 20 20 20 62   65 67 69 6E 0A 3C 01 03   .Á..   begin.<..
31627A20:  04 C3 08 20 35 02 C1 05   35 20 20 20 20 20 20 20   .Ã. 5.Á.5
31627A30:  20 72 65 74 75 72 6E 20   64 62 6D 73 5F 61 73 73    return dbms_ass
31627A40:  65 72 74 2E 65 6E 71 75   6F 74 65 5F 6E 61 6D 65   ert.enquote_name
31627A50:  28 73 74 72 2C 20 46 41   4C 53 45 29 3B 0A 3C 01   (str, FALSE);.<.
```

Figure 2-6. *Showing a deleted PL/SQL procedure in a datafile. Copyright (c) PeteFinnigan.com Limited. Used with permission.*

One of the big differences between the police analyzing a perpetrator's hard drive on a PC is that we are not looking for images or web access. We are trying to establish if an attacker has read data, or worse, has escalated privileges by creation of objects in the database or even changed settings in the database. This is much more complex than simply searching for text with grep like utilities.

The Oracle recycle bin and flashback (discussed in Chapter 2) are also good options if they are enabled for looking for deleted or modified data.

Tuning Tools

One of the bigger issues with collecting artifacts for forensic analysis is the lack of natural records for read access to data written by default by the database engine. Tuning tools, both built into the database and external, can help in this regard. Quite often DBAs will use the Oracle database's built-in tuning features, such as trace, to solve a performance problem.

The customer may have licensed the Oracle diagnostic pack and tuning pack. If the diagnostic pack and tuning pack is licensed, then the AWR and ASH repositories may be populated with data that includes SQL, timing, and bind data linked to database users.

Caution   Just because the Oracle diagnostic pack and tuning pack views always exist in the database does not mean that you can use them. Accessing the database views if you don't have a license incurs a license violation could cost your company a lot of money. The contents of these views may be your last hope in investigation; fully check out the license implications first before you query contents of these views.

Base tables and views such as:

```
WRI$_ADV_SQLW_STMTS
WRHS$_SQLTEXT
WI$_STATEMENT
WRH$_SQLTEXT
DBA_HIST_SQLTEXT
DBA_WI_STATEMENTS
DBA_SQLSET_STATEMENTS
WRH$_ACTIVE_SESSION_HISTORY
```

For instance, DBA_HIST_SQLTEXT contained a column called SQL_TEXT that holds captures of SQL taken on a periodic basic from the V$SQL view. The view WRH$_ACTIVE_SESSION_HISTORY also shows history of connections to the database that could be useful if auditing is not enabled for connections. There are more views and tables as part of AWR and ASH, that can be explored and that may contain information useful to a forensics analysis.

Third-party tools such as Quest spotlight or Quest Foglight may also have been purchased and implemented. These tools may also contain some historic SQL of interest and bind and link to database users or external identifiers. For instance, the Quest Spotlight product contains the view QUEST_SOO_AT_SQL_STMT_PIECES, which has a SQL statement pieces column. Spotlight also has a table called QUEST_PPCM_SQL_TEXT that contains a SQL_TEXT column and the QUEST_PPCM_CUSTOM_SQL table has also a SQL_TEXT column. These tables and more in any Quest product may prove useful in a forensic analysis review.

The database may also have STATSPACK installed as it still free but quite old. The STATSPACK (which stands for Statistics Package) is a simple utility to capture various information from the database on a periodic basis. These are known as snapshots. The captured data includes details such as database parameters, events, details and background events, details of the SGA, and of course SQL.

The STATS$SQL_SUMMARY table includes a SQL_TEXT column. The STATS$SQLTEXT table also has a SQL_TEXT column. In all of the tuning tools available SQL text is a valid commodity to use in a forensic analysis but other useful information is also available. For instance, the STATS$SQL_PLAN table includes details of SQL plans. This means that objects accessed as part of SQL are referenced in this table. The third-party tools and the Oracle tuning and diagnostic packs also include similar data. So even if it is not possible to see actual SQL that was executed, it may be possible via these tuning tools to understand the objects that were accessed as part of SQL or DML. Even database parameters could have been changed by an attacker. For instance, an attacker may want to disable the audit trail; in Oracle before 12c and indeed in 12c if using mixed mode the audit trail is enabled and disabled by setting an initialization parameter. If an attacker was able to get SYSDBA or DBA access, then he may have been able to change the parameter and stop and restart the database. If tools such as STATSPACK or the tuning pack were enabled, then historic settings of parameters may be included. This could also help a forensic investigation.

There are also a number of free tools used for tuning that come from third parties or from Oracle support. Examples are MOATS and SNAPPER from Tanel Poder and SQLXPLAINT from Carlos Sierra (which is download from Oracle) who previously wrote and maintained the tool.

One of the key issues with free and commercial tuning tools is that to have useful forensics data contained within the repositories of these tools, they must have been set up to capture the data you are interested in. The primary function of a tuning tool is of course to tune the database, not to provide forensics information. A forensics investigation should also include searching for any tuning tools that may be installed and establishing if any relevant data has been captured that would be useful to the investigation.

Bear in mind the license arrangements of some of these tools. Be careful not to view the repository information facilities tools if they require a license, as that would be a license infringement.

Rootkits

What is a *rootkit*? A rootkit is made up of the words *root* and *kit*. The word *root* being the name of the superuser in Unix and the word *kit* being the idea that a set of tools is needed in a so-called rootkit. The traditional purpose of a rootkit used on a Unix server or Windows box is to allow an attacker to remain on the server as a privileged user undetected. The rootkit would include tools to hide his presence on the server and tools to allow him to regain access as a superuser should he be locked out. These ways back in are traditionally called backdoors. A hacker in general installs new versions of commands and tools that satisfy these two requirements; a way back in and hiding his every move. An example of hiding could be that he replaces the Unix who and ps commands with commands that do not show his user identity if used by the real system administrator logged in as root.

The idea of rootkits in Oracle was first suggested in approximately 2005 when an Argentinean company offered for sale an Oracle rootkit for vendors of Oracle security database activity monitoring, intrusion detection, and vulnerability scanning products. In 2006 Alexander Kornbrust and David Litchfield both presented papers on Oracle based rootkits at the BlackHat conferences in the United States and Europe.

Despite this initial interest and activity around Oracle rootkits, it has all gone very quiet for many years with no talks or papers specifically aimed at Oracle based rootkits.

An attack on a server that hosts an Oracle database is still a valid target for a rootkit to be installed by an attacker at the server level. Adding a viable rootkit that works at the Oracle level is much harder though.

Listing 2-22 shows how part of rootkit may be implemented in an Oracle database by an attacker. In this simple example he takes the source code of the DBA_USERS view and adds an extra line to the view definition. He excludes his user called HACKER from being returned in queries against this view.

Listing 2-22. A Simple Example of How a User May Be Hidden in an Oracle Database

```
SQL> set pages 55
SQL> set long 1000000
SQL> select text from dba_views
  2  where view_name='DBA_USERS';

TEXT
-----------------------------------------------------------------
select u.name, u.user#,
     decode(u.password, 'GLOBAL', u.password,
                        'EXTERNAL', u.password,
                        NULL),
     m.status,
```

```
    decode(mod(u.astatus, 16), 4, u.ltime,
{...}
    and dp.resource#=1
    and pr.type# = 1
    and pr.resource# = 1
    and u.name<>'HACKER'
```

There is a major flaw in this very simple type of rootkit; the DBA could simply list out users from SYS.USER$ and the hackers user would be visible again. The other big problem is that there are many hundreds of other views that could also reveal hacker's user—some views having the same column name as DBA_USERS and some having different column names such as the OWNER column in DBA_OBJECTS or DBA_PROCEDURES if the hacker also created any objects. Hundreds of views would need to be changed quickly to successfully hide the hacker but it would still be visible in base dictionary tables.

A number of types of rootkits were suggested for Oracle back in the 2005/2006 timeframe. These included this simple example by editing system views and more complex rootkits by editing the Oracle binaries and changing all references to SYS.USER$ to SYS.AUSER$ and creating a copy of the user table in the database. This was very complex and messy and would require the database to be shut down to relink all of the binaries. Other suggestions involved pinning packages to the SGA where the package had been already removed, therefore hiding the functionality. It was also suggested by Denis Yurichev to use traditional operating system rootkit approaches and hook the user function in the Oracle binary.

Is it realistic that you would find a rootkit in an Oracle database that you are investigating? In reality, probably not, but you should not discount rootkits completely. The ideas for rootkits have been around for more than 10 years, so it's possible that someone could install a rootkit in an Oracle database. There are no comprehensive rootkits for Oracle freely available on the Internet, so attackers have to have written their own rootkits.

Is it possible to detect a rootkit in an Oracle database? For simple rootkits such as the example shown in Listing 2-22 the answer is yes; in fact, commercial Oracle vulnerability scanning tools such as PFCLScan do provide checks to detect this type of rootkit. The second type of rootkit where the Oracle binary has been changed and an additional SYS.USER$ table has been added are also tested for a commercial tools such as PFCLScan. So, yes it is possible to detect rootkits and a simplistic check could be used with an SQL query that compares the number of users in the SYS.USER$ table with that in the DBA_USERS view. Listing 2-23 shows a simple SQL-based check that can detect if the view DBA_USERS may have been modified as part of a rootkit.

As part of any incident response and forensic analysis, we should not ignore rootkits completely and at least a simple check should be made to establish if any simplistic rootkit was installed. Detecting rootkits could be done in a number of possible ways within the Oracle database.

A time-based check could be used for any dictionary views that have a different timestamp from the other core views. For instance, if the database was installed on 1st March 2010 and there have been no upgrades or changes that require recompilation of views then the timestamps of all of the core views such as DBA_USERS or V$SESSION or V$PROCESS should be on or around 1st March 2010. If some views have a much more recent timestamp then the source code of the view can be investigated. In reality, dictionary views will change every time there is a patch of an upgrade or anything that requires recompilation of views, so this may not be a reliable method.

Listing 2-23 shows an example of a different type of check, which is for detecting a change to the views DBA_USERS and ALL_USERS. It is simply an account of users in these two views with a comparison to SYS.USER$. Even this check is not simple, as the base table also stores details of roles. The type of the record in this table is defined by the TYPE# column. In older versions of Oracle, this column had one of two values—a 1 or a 0.

This indicated whether the record was a role or a user. Since edition-based redefinition was added, this column can also include different values because of the edition—this should be considered.

Listing 2-23. A Simple Check for an Oracle Rootkit

```
SQl > select name from sys.user$ where type#=1
  2   minus
  3   select username from dba_users;

no rows selected

SQL> select name from sys.user$ where type#=1
  2   minus
  3   select username from all_users;

no rows selected

SQL>
```

An alternative check for a rootkit would be to have a predefined list of checksums for every object of relevance in the database. This would initially include views and procedures. This list of checksums would need to be stored outside of the database so that it couldn't be manipulated and the list could be used to re-checksum every object and compare it to the list. Maintenance of this list would become very tiresome, as each new release of the database and every patch could potentially change a view definition of PL/SQL code. Therefore, the master checksums would need to be recalculated and stored on ongoing basis. This is not practical unless you have resource available to do this.

For the really paranoid, if checksums are used via packages in the database such as DBMS_UTILITY then it's essential that the checksum utility also be validated if you're using it to test for rootkits.

CHAPTER 3

Incident Response Approach

If you are unlucky enough to have a confirmed breach of your Oracle database or even a potential breach and you have no plan of what to do, dealing with it will become very ad hoc and likely cost much more money and take much more time than it should. Planning for an incident response is the most important part of the process and indeed this is the most important chapter of the whole book. If you plan, then you will know what to do, the right person will lead you, and you will have the right team involved in the process and have the right tools in your toolbox. Most importantly, you will also have the correct knowledge to deal with the incident.

It is vital to create and document the incident response process. This should be a formal process that is signed off on and agreed by all relevant parties in the organization. This document or plan can then be used as a step-by-step guide to deal with the incident.

In advance of an incident, someone must be identified as the incident coordinator. This is the person who will lead the response. There should also be an incident response team who will be led by the incident coordinator. The team should have the right balance of skills—including security skills, management skills, and Oracle skills. It is also important to pre-build a toolkit to be used as part of a response. This chapter explores all these ideas.

© Pete Finnigan 2018
P. Finnigan, *Oracle Incident Response and Forensics*,
https://doi.org/10.1007/978-1-4842-3264-4_3

Planning

It should go without saying that planning must be the first step toward a viable incident response process. Simply acknowledging that a breach might occur and you have to deal with it is not enough. You must create a detailed plan that shows exactly who will be involved and what they must do if a breach occurs. This plan should be documented and agreed on and signed off by all relevant parties, ideally with budget owners and business owners. It is important that everyone in the company take the threat of a data breach very seriously.

In the UK and across the EU, there is a new data protection law to be launched in May 2018. This new GDPR law will demand better, more secure handling of personal data. Companies even outside of the EU, if they process EU citizens' data, will need to comply with GDPR. This new law means that you must know when you have been breached. You must know which individual records were accessed (or most likely accessed) as part of the breach. You must report the breach within so many hours of it occurring or potentially you may pay enormous fines. The new law, similar to other laws around the world for data protection, also requires you to know where that data is stored within your systems. It must be possible for that data to be extracted in a standard format to be given to the person who it refers to if requested formally. Also, GDPR introduced a new concept, which is the right to be forgotten. This means someone whose data you process can demand that you delete that data. That can become very complex, especially as with an Oracle data is never really deleted but simply marked as space that can be reused.

These new regulations, certainly in the UK and the EU, combined with the upsurge of data breaches over recent years will require that companies know what to do if their database has been breached. They must know how to identify if a breach has occurred and they must know how to analyze and investigate that breach. This means it is imperative to plan in advance for a potential breach; hopefully, one will never occur.

The planning must include a documented step-by-step process. It must include the nomination of a leader of the process. It must also include identification of a suitable team to deal with the breach. This chapter explores this in more detail.

Create an Incident Response Approach

An incident response process must not be ad hoc in nature. The process must be formally documented so that it can be signed off and agreed to in advance. It also means that the budget should be made available to deal with a response so that normal business can be halted temporarily if necessary and the team can spring into action to start to investigate and deal with the breach.

The process does not need to be complex; in fact, it should be a succinct as possible so that it is easy to follow without any question. The process should identify the risk that the investigation team may be involved with the original breach. For instance, if the investigation was simply handed to the DBA and he's told get on with it and report back when you discovered how the database was breached, then there could be a major problem if it was in fact the DBA who stole the data and sold it online to criminal proponents. This does not mean that the DBA cannot be involved with the investigation; it simply means that someone is clearly unbiased. Ideally more than one person controls the process to ensure that it is safe and trustworthy.

Incident response approach should ideally be a checklist with some header information. The header information can be identification and mobilization of the relevant team members or substitutes if the identified people no longer work in the company and cannot be moved into the incident response team on an instant basis.

The leader can use the document, as a checklist, to make sure that every step of the process is followed and that it is ticked off as it's complete.

Spend some time in advance creating your own incident response process or documentation. My advice is that this should fit on a single sheet of paper and attached to a clipboard so it can be easily ticked off as it's completed. This chapter presents information about team members and the leader and tools that should be used and presents the steps that could be part of your incident response process. Feel free to use the steps defined here; I have used these steps at a number of customer sites in the development of incident response processes and used them to respond to incidents where the customer did not have a preplanned incident response process or team.

The process is presented as a bulleted list in this chapter, but feel free to convert it into a table or a ticklist.

It is most important that the process is documented and signed off in advance.

Incident Coordinator

A single person should be appointed to lead the incident response process. The choice of who this person is can be difficult. In some organizations where the IT team is very small, creating a team to deal with an incident is difficult because it means that most likely every member of the IT team will be part of it. In an organization that is very small, it is unlikely there is any spare resource to simply put on standby for incident responses. It is also unlikely that there is already an Oracle security person. In every organization, large or small, there is likely to be some element of a security team. In large organizations, the scope is much greater to predefine relevant people to lead an incident.

Whether the team available to deal with a response is large or small; in other words the resources available within your company are large or small, it make senses that the incident coordinator or leader be a person of trust. In any incident response it is more likely that the attacker is internal and works at the organization. It is also likely that the attacker has knowledge of the data that has been stolen and has knowledge of the technical infrastructure; in other words, he knows where to find what he wants to steal. It's quite obvious that somebody who works for you (with knowledge and a desktop PC and possibly Oracle database-related applications) has a much easier chance of stealing data.

It makes sense to ensure that the person leading the investigation cannot manipulate the investigation should they be involved with the original breach. Therefore, it makes sense to appoint somebody outside of the IT team and outside of the normal business processing of the data that was stolen. If the coordinator in general does not have knowledge of the data that has been stolen, and that person in general does not have the credentials to access the database or indeed data applications installed on his or her PC, they are less likely to have been involved in the original breach. There is no 100% guarantee that the person leading the investigation was not involved, but it makes sense to reduce this risk as much as possible. To that end, if resources allow, it's sensible to ensure someone else moderates the coordinator.

All businesses are complex and busy and people take vacations, so it also makes sense to ensure that substitutes are also identified. In a large company, it most likely makes sense to identify three or four coordinators and teams, depending on where the investigation takes place and on which data.

But at least identify one person who is able to lead the process and then identify at least one substitute should that person not be available. That person needs to lead the process and follow the list without being forced to change the process dynamically. A person does not need to be a security expert or an Oracle expert; they simply need to be able to manage people to follow the list. That said, security knowledge would be useful, as would Oracle knowledge to understand what other people are doing and that the results are trustworthy. Ideally, the coordinator should receive training in areas that are relevant to this task, such as security or Oracle, but this is not mandatory.

The important points are that an incident coordinator must be identified in advance of a potential breach and this person should not be biased toward other agendas. If the coordinator has the freedom to investigate, a more reliable result will be obtained.

Create an Incident Response Team

The incident response coordinator should be unbiased and trustworthy and ideally chosen because of the unlikelihood of being involved with a breach, but unfortunately the rest of the team needs to have skills relevant to the system being investigated or business knowledge of the area of breach. Each of these people must be untrustworthy. There is no simple solution to this problem of untrustworthiness other than ensuring multiple people are involved so that a cover-up would require collusion on a much larger scale, which should be less likely but not impossible.

The team members should have a number of skills and ideally have more than one person in each skill area. As stated, this could help prevent collusion but also ensures that more than one person is available should a breach occur.

What sort of skills are required? Because of the complex nature of an Oracle database and the fact that it is a security investigation, the ideal person would be someone with Oracle security skills. The detailed skills necessary in the area of security and Oracle are less likely to exist in most companies in one person. Usually, there will be a security team or at least a security person, but unless the company is large, this is unlikely to be a person with specific Oracle security skills in the security department. Similarly with the DBA team, the staff is likely to have detailed knowledge of Oracle, but less likely to have detailed knowledge of Oracle security.

In general, over many years it has been concluded that it is simpler to teach an Oracle person security skills than teach a security person Oracle skills. The concepts of security are much simpler than the inordinate amount of knowledge needed to understand Oracle.

The skills needed should include:

- **Security person**: Should have the knowledge of breaches, possibly incident responses, and techniques used by hackers to gain access to systems. This is likely to be in the areas of operating systems and possibly firewalls. This person should bring a security perspective to the analysis process.

- **Oracle person (DBA)**: Most likely a DBA who has enough knowledge of the Oracle database to be able to control it, shut it down, remove users or sessions, and be able to locate information from within the Oracle database as requested, and in conjunction with the security person.

- **Businessperson**: Someone from the business area, ideally outside of IT but involved with the day-to-day running of the business processes hosted by the Oracle database that has been attacked. This person should have good knowledge of the data held in the database, understand which data is most valuable, and be able to recognize normal processing and abnormal processing as presented by the security person.

- **Management person**: A person who has the ability to make decisions that affect budget or cost must be part of the team. Often, investigation quick decisions are needed that may cost money to implement. For instance, in a recent forensic investigation that I took part in, we realized that additional systems had almost certainly been compromised by the attacker. A decision needed to be made quickly to allow me to investigate those systems as well.

- **Public relations**: It is important to consider public relations as part of the response. A lack of information given out once an incident has become public serves to enrage the victims. A person should be appointed as a single point of contact with any form of media. This could be posting a message on Twitter or Facebook or on the company web site or it could even involve giving an interview on television. No other person should be allowed to discuss the incident either verbally or in writing on any platform. Management and the incident coordinator should approve any statement given out by the public relations person.

The team should be as small as possible to avoid business by committee. One of the reasons to have a process that is documented is so that everyone can follow the process step-by-step and ensure that every step is completed and no additional unnecessary steps are added. Still, in the investigation of a complex Oracle database, it is likely that the amount of investigation, artifact collection, and forensic analysis are unknown quantities in advance. The team needs to be flexible in terms of time and size. It is useful to identify a single person for each role but also identify substitutes if necessary. The substitute may be used if someone else is not available and can assist when additional resources are needed.

If necessary, in advance of any potential investigation, some level of training is needed for the team and potential additional team members who may become part of an investigation. Initially this training should at least be to review the complete process and to ensure that everyone understands the steps involved and what is needed from them during an investigation. This type of training can be performed internally and is led by a security person.

Create an Incident Response Process

The incident response process must be documented. Ideally, this should be as succinct as possible so as to make following it simple. In the event of an alert, the incident response/resolution process must be worked through completely. Part of the incident response process should be a communication channel. There should be a recognized method within the organization of raising or alerting an incident. A method to implement this can be different in each organization. A simple solution is to create an e-mail address whose purpose it is to receive notification of any incident. This e-mail address can be public so that any member of the public can raise an incident response in the organization. This is not the ideal way to learn about an incident, but it is still valid. Internally, any incident that's feared to have happened should also be reported to the same e-mail address.

The incident coordinator and/or his substitute should manage the incident response e-mail. Notices should be given out to the whole organization with a short training session to make everyone in the organization aware of how to deal with a potential incident. If incidents are reported in an ad hoc way to different departments of the company and some departments attempt to investigate without any structure, some departments may simply ignore the issue and other departments may publicly leak the breach.

Consistency is very important. Ensure that every member of the organization understands that any potential breach could be very damaging to the company. Everyone should understand that while keeping a breach quiet is not ethical in terms of not telling the victims, it is important to ensure that the breaches are handled and reported on correctly to the media and especially through social media.

This process should include the following steps:

- **Identify the incident response leader**: This step falls outside the process, as the incident response leader or coordinator should already be assigned in advance of any potential incident. Any subordinates or substitutes must also be identified in advance. This should always be someone available who can step in and manage an incident.

- **Recognize that an alert has occurred**: There should be a central reporting point for any potential incident. This could be an e-mail address, but it doesn't have to be. The main objective is to ensure that all reports of a breach are funneled to one source. Any report arriving at the source should be treated seriously and investigated to understand if it really is a breach. For instance, data that has been posted to a web site such as Dropbox or Twitter can be easily analyzed to see if it did come from the Oracle database. If an alert has not been raised through a reporting system, then assessing whether a breach has occurred becomes much harder. The breach could be noticed due to strange behavior of an employee. In this case, the person who notices the strange behavior should use the same breach notification process. Perhaps the breach or potential breach is noticed through standard business reporting. Perhaps something changes or is missing or additional accounts exist in the database that weren't there yesterday. Perhaps the DBA comes to work and notices that additional accounts were approved. Again, these types of incidents should be reported to the same channel. Some breaches may not come initially as a notice to an e-mail address or other notification system, but inevitably any initial suspicion should be raised through the official channel.

- **Control passes to the incident response leader**: Once a breach has been confirmed, control of the process should pass to the incident response leader. He should then ensure that a breach is officially recognized and that the incident response process is live. The incident controller should then have the final say on any next steps. He should have the ability to overrule the business or management whose first response may be to keep the business running and ignore the incident.

- **Do not turn off the database or disconnect from the network (at this stage)**: An initial reaction may be to disconnect the machine from the network or to power it down or, even worse, unplug the power cord. Unplugging the power cord to a large Oracle database server could be catastrophic. (It perhaps wouldn't shut it down anyway if it had redundant power sources.) Although Oracle is much more reliable than it was in the old days, turning the database power off can still cause it to be corrupted. Pulling the power on the server can also cause the server to be corrupted. The most important issue is that any live data that could possibly be gathered from the database server or from the database itself will be lost; the worst-case scenario is at the machine itself is lost. Do not disconnect the server from the network, do not disconnect the database from the network, and do not shut it down. Stopping the attacker from doing anything else may be a good idea, but destroying potential transient evidence is probably worse.

- **Investigate if the attack is real**: At this point, the incident response leader should appoint someone on the team, depending on what the breach is, to investigate as to whether it really is a breach. In the case of data posted on the Internet, somebody in the team could look into the database and understand which tables the data came from. Perhaps someone will confirm that that data should not be on the Internet; therefore, there is a verified breach. It is important that all potential breaches be investigated, even if they turn out not to be a breach. The old case of crying wolf should not come into play; it's better to cry wolf sometimes and be on top of an issue as soon as possible.

- **Document the system**: Photograph the system, particularly the maker's plate serial numbers and other relevant data. If the threat was conducted internally, a photograph the perpetrator desk's can be very helpful in finding evidence in the surrounding area.

- **Perform incident response (collect live data)**: Perform the steps to collect the volatile and transient data from the database server. This includes the timestamps, users logged in, processes running, ports open, files open, and more. Perform the necessary steps to gather copies of all the server log files. Gather all database log files, trace files, and configuration files. Gather logs from other relevant servers or clients. This includes web server logs and application server logs. Perform live analysis of the database engine to obtain the live, transient data or volatile data from the database. This includes SQL that is currently in the

SGA, date and timestamps, processes and sessions, connected users, running SQL, and more.

- **Perform incident response (collect less volatile data)**: Gather all further forensic evidence from the database. This includes all users, password hashes, privileges for users, all membership of roles, all external accesses (files, network, and links), jobs, audit trails, evidence from the cost-based optimizer, evidence from the library cache, and much more.

- **Break the network connection to the database**: Breaking the connection will prevent any new network based access to the database. This will not prevent direct access from the server itself, which at this stage should only be done by the incident response team. The database is not shut down, so transient data is still available if necessary; the database is not in danger of being corrupted by the shutdown process.

- **Copy hard disks and evidence**: Where possible, make byte for byte copies of any hard disk that is relevant to the database server. Or make copies of individual evidence where possible.

- **Checksum the evidence**: Ensure all evidence that is collected is checksummed in the source storage before removed and the checksums are stored independently. This allows the evidence to be re-checksum It's then compared to the stored value to prove that it's the same data that is being analyzed.

- **Perform forensic analysis of the data**: Using the live data, the server data, external data, and the data from the database itself, start to perform forensic analysis. The analysis should start from the point of the confirmed breach. If the breach is confirmed, there should be evidence to corroborate that breach. This evidence should also have timestamp details. This gives the first start time of the breach; use the last access time by normal users as the end date of the breach. The start the breach may be pushed back as more evidence is analyzed. Attempt to locate evidence that corroborates the access by the attacker and locates his access.

- **Build a timeline of events**: Build a timeline based on the start time and the end time of all actions that are relevant and that occurred in the database, on the server, and on external servers such as web servers. Use this timeline evidence to build an understanding of what the attacker did. This should include how he got in, who was he connected as, what he saw, what he did, what privileges he had, and what he could have done with more skill.

- **Shut down and restore**: Decide whether to shut down the database at this point. If the database is mission-critical, this decision will need to be balanced against business needs. Before the decision is made to shut down and restore the database, you must understand what the attacker did. It is important to know if the data is compromised. If the data was just read and no objects were created and there no escalation of duties, most likely, the data is not actually corrupt; it has just been stolen. In this instance, with careful analysis, it is probably acceptable not to restore the system. Restoring the system would involve the need to restore to either a point in time before the attack took place and then reapplying all of the business after that point to restore to the current time. If the restored database had any corruptions caused by the attacker, these will be replayed into a restored version of the production database. In some systems it is probably more practical to fully understand what the attack did, restore the system to a clean state but the same point in time and then reversed the actions of the attacker. In this way, lost business is kept to a minimum and the need to reapply business manually is kept to a minimum.

- **Document the attack**: It is important to document the process and all of the evidence that was captured. Furthermore, document your understanding of what happened. This includes all the actions the attacker took and an indication of any data that he saw or potentially stole. This report should also aim to identify the gaps in the system that allowed the attacker to enter in the first place and perhaps to escalate his permissions once he was in the system. The conclusions of the report should not only aim to understand exactly what the attacker did, but also identify the weaknesses and suggest how to fix them.

- **Report the issue**: Reporting the issue is not simple as it sounds. First of all, it depends on the type of attack. If the attack involved data loss, there is probably a bigger requirement to disclose. If the attack involved misuse or destruction or excess rights, it may depend on other factors. If there are regulations that govern your industry or general regulations such as PCI or GDPR, you will be required to report the issue of data loss. If your industry is not governed by any data regulations, then maybe there isn't even someone to report the breach to. If you work for an ethical company and customer data has been lost, yet there is no requirement to report it, you should consider whether you should still inform customers anyway; it's ethically correct to do so.

Note   One of the biggest issues in analyzing an Oracle database is the more you investigate inside the database, the more it changes the database itself. Providing the access is read-only, this should only really change the transient data within the SGA. Unfortunately, almost every action in the database, even including SELECT statements, can generate changes to dictionary records. For instance, if auditing were enabled on a particular database view, and as part of the analysis, you access that, an audit record would be created. The creation of the audit record would also involve more changes to the SGA, as the INSERT statement into the AUD$ table is compiled and processed.

You should aim to answer a number of questions during the investigation:

- **Did an attack actually occur?** You need to establish that the initial evidence does actually point to an attack having taken place. This is the first proof that is needed and is also reported in the final documentation

- **How did the attacker gain access?** It is imperative to understand exactly how the attacker gained access to the database. Was it via a web application, perhaps via SQL Injection, or perhaps was it a DBA who accessed personal data to save and later sell. Without understanding exactly how the attacker gained access, you cannot begin to understand exactly what privileges he had and what he could have done as well as what he did do. You need this information to be able to lock down and secure the database.

- **Who did the attacker gain access as?** Which database user did the attacker use to gain access. Was the access direct using a tool such as SQL*Plus, or was the connection indirect via SQL Injection through a web application? In this case, the web server logs into the database and the attacker piggybacks on to that user. In some cases, the potential actions of the attacker are perhaps more limited by a web-based access than they would be by direct access. Some attacks may start as web-based access and the attacker may then be able to download and install command-line tools or graphical tools to make a direct connection to the database and browse.

- **What was the "reach" of his access?** What rights and privileges are granted to the user that the attacker used? This will give you a clear picture of the functionality and the data that the attacker could have accessed. This is the maximum access possible for the particular database user, but it may be that something like a web-based application that limits the attacker's use of the potential access and rights.

- **What could he have done if he had more skills?**
  An attacker with more skill may find a way to further
  elevate the privileges within the database. An unskilled
  or very semiskilled attacker may use off-the-shelf
  tools to initiate a brute force access to a database via a
  vulnerable web site URL. A skilled hacker may be able
  to tunnel further attacks through the initial attack. An
  example is finding SQL Injection that allows the calling
  of a procedure. Perhaps the procedure could then be
  used to further inject DDL. This means that an attacker
  can do anything as the user that he is connected to.
  He could inject code as DDL into a procedure call,
  which is itself injected into vulnerable SQL as SQL
  Injection. This generally would require a much higher
  level of skill. So while an attacker may have access to
  a certain set of privileges, not all hackers will have the
  skill to take advantage of this. In some cases, the hacker
  may be able to gain elevated privileges by exploiting
  vulnerabilities in PL/SQL in the database that runs
  a higher-level user. If this were possible, the attacker
  may then be able to gain access to other databases by
  database links or the operating system of the server or
  potentially gain access to the server as the Oracle user.
  To analyze the possibilities, you need some level of
  knowledge of Oracle security and potential database
  hacking. Also bear in mind that in Oracle 12.2.0.1, there
  are tens of thousands of public privileges available to
  any database user; in general, most of these are execute
  privileges.

The investigation should not change the database. Some documents suggest that a superuser such as SYS be used for forensic analysis. Although it makes sense to use an existing user, there is a risk that when a powerful user is used, changes could be made to the database nefariously. Creating a user specifically for the investigation in one sense would be ideal because the privileges granted to it could be limited to as read-only as possible this would not work. Creating a user in a compromised database would certainly change the database. Adding a user involves many SQL actions, so it could corrupt the SGA at least and potentially change the dictionary by adding objects to it. This should be avoided. So in retrospect, even though a user such as SYS is dangerous because it can change the database, it makes more sense to use this type of user to gain access to everything without difficulty. Just bear in mind that the database could be changed or evidence could be deleted.

Can the evidence extracted from the database be trusted or verified? This is very difficult to answer. Of course, using SYS means that anything in the database can be changed. Some of the artifacts that are removed from the database should be checksummed to ensure that they can be validated at a later date if that same data is accessed again. This process of creating a checksum would invariably use a package in the database such as DBMS_SQLHASH, but this package could also have been modified by the attacker or the investigator. An extremely thorough investigation should validate that any of the tools used in the investigation have not been corrupted or changed.

An attacker could also change views in the database to hide the actions of the database objects that he created. This is called a *root kit.* Gathering evidence from database views is therefore also susceptible to a trust problem. A view is a compiled piece of SQL that is present in the database to easy access to multiple tables that already include a predicate (where clause). Attackers can easily change these views to add SQL in the predicate. The analysis of the database should take this into account and either one of two actions can be taken. The first is to only use the base tables in the data dictionary so as to avoid using views that could have been changed. The second is to validate the views first to ensure they haven't been changed and then use views to access the data dictionary as part of the analysis and data gathering.

Validating the views in one sense is simple. You take a checksum of each view and then compare that with a known valid database. The problem with this is that the source code of views can change between platforms and patches. To validate the views, you must maintain an exact copy of the same database version to be able to generate the same checksums in it to use as a comparison. This would be tedious.

Choosing between direct access or using views must be decided carefully.

The issue of public relations must be considered. If someone external reports the breach to you, then someone external already knows you have been breached and could be talking to the press or media or disclosing it on social media or similar. If the story gets out first, then you need to have a response that shows you care and you are doing something about it to limit the damage as much as possible. It is very important that a single contact is appointed within your own organization to speak to the media to post on social media any updates. Managing public relations and media access is a very important part of incident response. Don't lie to the media or in statements that you make. Don't be overoptimistic about your progress or about the level of the incident. If it's likely that an attacker could have taken 100,000 records but you feel he might have taken 10, don't report immediately to the media that only 10 records were breached. This would be foolish if it later turned out that 100,000 records were available on Dropbox. Measure your interaction with the media guardedly. Never rush to make a statement; ensure that all the facts are straight first and then speak to the media.

Create and Collate a Toolkit

As part of the preparations to deal with an incident, you must source and build a toolkit. This toolkit should ideally be documented; this doesn't mean that detailed instructions need to be produced or sourced for every item in the toolkit, but a high-level list of what each tool does will be sufficient. It also makes sense that anyone who is involved in the incident response process know how to run the tools. Any supporting software that you need must also be sourced. Ideally, the toolkit should be copied to a CD or a DVD so that it is read-only and therefore cannot be altered before use. A more modern equivalent is use a pen drive or USB stick, but these are in general read-write, so don't satisfy the read-only aspect. Some USB sticks can be made read-only, so investigate this as a potential repository. If you use a FAT file system that doesn't support permissions, then this is not possible. If you use an NTFS file system, this can be done. Windows supports a tool called DISKPART; start this tool by typing diskpart and you will be left with the DISKPART> prompt. Now type the following after the prompt:

```
DISKPART> SELECT DISK "1"
```

where "1" is the drive that you want to protect. Then type the following after the prompt:

```
DISKPART> ATTRIBUTES DISK SET READONLY
```

This will make the USB drive read-only. Bear in mind that a USB drive was never intended to be protected, as the protection can just as easily be turned off again. Some USB drives include a mechanical switch, but this can be easily turned on or off

A sensible approach is to checksum all of the tools on the USB drive. A set of checksums can then be stored for comparison when the tools are used to prove that they are the same copies and have not been modified.

Each relevant member of the team should gain experience with the tools ahead of any potential breach. It is important to understand what a tool does and how it behaves in advance of having to use it. They must understand what the output looks like under normal circumstances, so that when a breach occurs, they will understand the difference when actual evidence shows up.

Creating a toolkit for Oracle forensics can be a problem because at this point in time there are no specific commercial Oracle security forensics tools available. But this is about to change, as there is one commercial product coming soon. PFCLScan version 2.0 (see `http://www.petefinnigan.com/products/pfclscan.htm` for details of the features and the pricing), which will be released by the time you have this book in your hands. It will include an update over the current version 1.9 that adds four new Oracle forensics project templates for use in helping Oracle incident response and forensics analysis, as well for use in auditing your database for security vulnerabilities.

The first project template shown in Figure 3-1, to be used in the interview section, will allow an incident coordinator to manage the incident response process through PFCLScan and therefore generate reports against this process. There are live and static incident response projects to allow volatile data collection and less volatile data collection using PFCLScan from the database. The fourth and final prebuilt project template will allow analysis of the static and volatile data collection projects. This project will be driven by a start and end date and will allow the user to build a timeline from all of the collected artifacts and highlight issues that could be relevant to an attack.

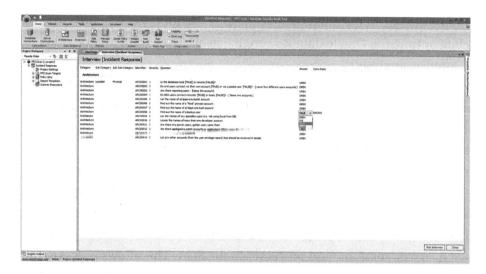

Figure 3-1. *A question and answer type project in PFCLScan. Copyright (c) PeteFinnigan.com Limited. Used with permission.*

The PFCLScan was the first commercial tool that had Oracle forensics built into it. In 2007, David Litchfield announced he was developing a tool called FEDS, but it was never released. Then in 2011, David created a company called V3rity and released some small command-line tools, which have since disappeared. No commercial tool was ever released despite the company being acquired.

The good news is that you don't necessarily need commercial tools or specific tools such as those developed by David Litchfield to analyze Oracle data files. Standard Oracle, tools such as SQL*Plus, will work just fine with a set of simple PL/SQL and SQL queries.

Analyzing the server can involve existing forensic tools such as EnCase from Guidance software (see https://www.guidancesoftware.com/encase-forensic for more details).

You can use other tools from Oracle, such as redo analysis using LogMinor. There are also exotic options, such as oradebug or BBED to access the SGA or data blocks in memory directly. Little help is available online for tools such as oradebug or BBED, so these are not really

115

suitable outside of the hands of an expert. These tools were created to debug or tune the Oracle database engine itself. They were not intended for forensic analysis.

Miladin Modrakovic wrote a paper in 2004 based on Kyle Hailey's original work on direct SGA access in C. This work was intended to allow access to the SGA for tuning purposes. This paper can be found at `http://www.petefinnigan.com/Storing_Data_Directly_From_Oracle_SGA.pdf`. This is because it is possible to poll structures in the SGA extremely quickly using direct memory access and the C language. Doing the same in SQL is too slow. The same ideas can be used for Oracle forensics by writing a C program to access transient and volatile data such as SQL, users, sessions, and processes in the SGA. This allows access to the transient data without affecting the transient data. The big problem with this approach is that a different C program is needed for each operating system that supports Oracle. And each version of Oracle potentially changes the location of the X$ structures that make up the SGA. This would be a minefield to maintain.

Some tuning tools such as the tuning pack and diagnostic pack from Oracle (additional license required) allow monitoring and historic data to be collected from the SGA. Third-party tools such as foglight and spotlight from Quest operate in a similar way and again demand a license fee. These tools are intended for tuning, but they may prove useful in forensic analysis. There are also free tools available, such as SQLXPLAINT from Oracle and a tool such as snapper and MOATS from Tanel Poder. All of these may prove useful in forensic analysis but they are not intended for forensics.

The simplest approach is to gather the relevant log files and configuration files from Oracle with simple tools such as `ssh` and `sftp`. Manual analysis of these log files will suffice combined with simple grep or search commands. In terms of database analysis, SQL and simple PL/SQL scripts are the best approach. These are ubiquitous and will work on all supported platforms and versions of Oracle. The scripts need not be complex, as they gather simple sets of data from the database. This includes gathering volatile data from the SGA and more permanent data from the data dictionary of the database. Microsoft Office products such as Excel are really useful for sorting and analyzing data that has been gathered from the database. Excel also provides graphing facilities to visualize the patterns in data

Ensure that you pre-gather a suitable set of tools or scripts to allow artifacts to be taken from the database and subsequently analyzed. Is important to ensure you're familiar and trained with these tools.

The next chapter discusses some of the tools that provide more help.

CHAPTER 4

Reacting to an Incident

This chapter explores the scenarios involved in reacting to an incident. It focuses on the steps involved with incident response. This starts with a brief discussion of what not to do; it's important in advance to make sure that you don't make things worse by switching off the computer or the multi-node Oracle database server, for example. This would be completely impractical in any normal sense. The incident coordinator first verifies that an incident has actually occurred. Connecting to the system and verifying the system state are the next steps. In other words, you need to know exactly what was affected—versions, users who are connected, processes that are running, and other details that will be relevant at a later date when the analysis is used, perhaps in criminal proceedings. After an incident has been verified then a detailed analysis of the database needs to be done and this starts with artifact collection. The chapter includes with a brief discussion of whether to disconnect the database from the network and when and if to shut it down.

Artifacts must be collected in the correct order. Any collection that could affect the rest of the collection must be done first. One unfortunate problem with an Oracle database when using SQL as the incident response tool is that the act of running SQL can change the transient data of the database, so you must take care when collecting. Once the incident range has been established, the collection of the artifacts from the database can be made. This includes looking for changes to database objects, access to data, access to user accounts and elevated privileges and in general anything that can help coordinate the attack response.

A Sample Attack

Chapters 4 and 5 are based on a sample simulated attack of the simple company system supported by an Oracle database. The company runs two web-based applications. The first application supports the company's web site and uses a content management system to serve web pages to the public. This content management system uses an Oracle database as its data store. The intention of the public facing web site is to showcase the company's products and services and provide a blogging platform.

The second application supports the company's business processes. Employees of the company log into a web-based application that allows access to business-critical data. Authorized users are able to modify, delete, or add new suppliers, shipping information, customer details, products, and of course payment details such as credit cards. This application also uses a content management system with Oracle as its data store.

The biggest flaw in this company's database architecture is that it uses the same Oracle database to support the public facing web site and the business specific functionality. Even worse, the public facing web site data and backoffice business data are all stored in the same database schema; ORABLOG. The problems deepen as it also turns out that the public facing web site and the backoffice web application both connect to the database as the same schema owner; ORABLOG.

The attack was simulated of course for this book. Although it would be great to use evidence from a real customer's forensic analysis, no customer would agree to this. So instead we simulate an attack against a customer's web site supported by an Oracle database. A video was made of the actual attack and posted to my YouTube account. You can see it at `http://www.petefinnigan.com/forensics/hack.htm`. It is more interesting not to describe the details of the attack now, but instead leave that until after the forensic analysis in Chapter 5. Forensic analysis should be able to determine exactly what happened; that is the goal of course. After you've read the sample forensic analysis, you can watch the video to see what really happened.

What Not To Do

It is vital that the incident response process is planned carefully in advance. In an Oracle database, accessing the database itself can change the database. This was discussed in the last chapter. This means that we should read data from the database in a carefully pre-planned order so that limited changes or data corruption are likely to be made. It is also important to not immediately disconnect the database from the network or disconnect users or shut it down. We are dealing with production Oracle databases supporting a myriad of applications and simply turning the power off is not an option. Neither is disconnecting people, that is, without careful planning and forethought.

In simple terms, if an incident is raised then do not panic. Ensure that the process for incident response is worked through correctly. Ensure that the system is not touched so that live analysis can take place without corruption. Carefully consider the business requirements of the system—is the system compromised in terms of business integrity? Does it need to be completely rebuilt or can it be rectified after the analysis of the issue? One of the key tenets will be keeping the business running as smoothly as possible even when there has been a breach. So make no rash decisions straight away.

The first stage of incident response is to establish that an incident has in fact taken place. Once you verify the incident, the incident response team must jump into action. The incident coordinator must take the lead and ensure that the incident response process is followed step-by-step until completion.

This chapter focuses on collection of the incident-based artifacts from a sample database that has been exploited. This gives examples of some of the data they should collect and some sample queries to do just that.

Incident Verification and Identification

The first task is to verify that an incident has occurred. Establishing that an incident has in fact taken place is very complex. There is no golden bullet technique to do this. This is simply because one incident will not be the same as the next incident. Chapter 3 discussed planning for an incident and creating a team and a leader. You must also create an incident reporting channel. This could be as simple as an e-mail address so that the public or employees or customers can report an incident to you. If someone internally suspects an incident and makes initial investigations, then at some point they should also report the incident to the same channel. All employees of the company should be made aware of the incident response process so that they use it.

In real life, people don't always follow rules so expect that some incidents may start to occur and be investigated perhaps by members of the development team or the DBA team or even business people. Usually this is because someone notices something that is not normal and starts to investigate. It doesn't even need to be someone from IT; it could be a business person who noticed an anomaly in some figures or records that are normally processed. At some point, even with an ad hoc approach to investigating an incident, they must involve someone from IT or management.

Even if an incident comes to the attention of the correct people and not via the correct channel, the incident should be formally raised by someone to ensure standardization. However, the incident has been reported at some point it comes to the attention of the incident process team. This is the point at which someone must validate and verify that there really is an incident.

Some incidents will be easier to verify than others. For instance, if data for some of your customers held in your database has been posted on Dropbox or some attacker has announced publicly on social media that he has hacked your company's database and has taken data, then it's pretty much established already that it's genuine.

This should still be verified. The data must be obtained and then a search of the database must be made to establish whether this data really did come from the database. If the data that has been posted on Dropbox is posted with a certain order—for instance first name, last name, date of birth, e-mail address, postcode, first-line, second-line—then we have an order of columns that could have been extracted from a database table. Therefore, the first step is to do a search of the database to find every table that contains the type of information that has been stolen and to validate if any of the tables are located have the same order of data. It could be that the attacker selected the data in an order that is different from the structure of the table, but this is a starting point. If you can verify that the data did indeed come from that table because the order is the same, then you can verify the count of records in that table and compare it to the number of records that were stolen. If they match, then immediately you know that all records have been stolen. If they don't match, then perhaps the records came from a different system where the table does match but the system has less data. So perhaps the attacker gained access to a test system that is seven months old.

At the time the test system was populated with production data was used but in the seven months since the test system was populated more data has been added to the production system that is not in the test system. Compare the counts of records with other systems within your organization that copies data from the production system. This may give an indication of the exact database that the data was stolen from. If the data also included a timestamp for each record, then this may also indicate where the data came from and when. If data is added to a table on a daily basis and the data that has been exposed on the Internet has a final date for some record of three weeks ago, then almost certainly the data was taken three weeks ago.

At this point, it is also worth looking at a number of records that have been posted on the web site dropbox (if indeed this was the method that the attacker used) to establish whether the hacker took all of the data or just some of it. Just because he posted a subset of data to dropbox does not mean that he doesn't have all of the data.

In general, an attack falls into a number of broad categories:

- Data has been found outside of the company where it's clearly not normal or authorized.

- Something has happened that should not have. This could be a process running at the wrong time or access to a system out of hours or something similar.

- Something does not add up. There could be a discrepancy in summary reports that is not normally present, indicating that data may be corrupted or changed.

If the initial indication of an attack came from business employees, perhaps because they noticed some strange values in reports or a mismatch between banking records and invoices, then maybe the attack is more complex. Maybe an attacker managed to alter or change payment processing to steal money from your company. A clever technique could be that an employee changes the postal address for a customer in a company that lends money. This address change is made immediately before the payout check is sent and changed again immediately after this process; back to the original customers address of course.

Maybe an employee notices an inconsistency in invoices and payouts or perhaps notices an address in one record that doesn't match with another. The big problem with a breach is we don't know what the breach is until somebody thinks there is a breach, at which point we can start to investigate and dig into data. In this particular example, if there was auditing at the application layer, perhaps we can establish that an address was changed twice. An immediate response may be to check all the records to see if this action is common and that every customer's address has changed twice during the payout process. Visit this data and confirm employee addresses, as it's a good test to see if a breach has occurred.

Once you've establish that a breach has occurred or is in process, you need to establish some basic facts:

- *When did the attack start and end?* Sometimes it's possible to estimate this from date and timestamps on records that have been stolen or manipulated. It is often easier to establish the end date of an attack from timestamps or even the current date now at the start of the investigation. At this stage an initial guess as to the start of the attack can be made based on timestamps, perhaps comparisons between test systems and the production system to see if data is changed and when. The fact is, you need to establish the start date and the end date of the attack to use this as a basis in the analysis.

- *How did he get in?* The insertion point in to your systems by the attacker must be established. It's very important to understand how the attacker got in so that whatever method he used can be closed out and secured.

- *What did he steal or change?* A concerted effort must be made to establish exactly what was stolen or changed within the database. This gives a basis for assessing what to do with the database after the investigation is complete. If the complete range of actions that were made by the attacker are known, it may be possible to reverse those rather than completely rebuilding the database. This may give the opportunity to keep the system live rather than have downtime and manual rework or re-entry of data afterward.

- *What could the attacker have done?* By reviewing the privileges that the attacker had while he was in the database, you can assess the exact range of what he could have done. This might include what data he could have seen if he chose to, and which objects he could have deleted, changed, or accessed. Could he have escalated his privileges to another user or could he have access to the operating system or networking or even another database? This information can be used to help lock down and secure the database after the analysis is complete.

The type of attack can vary from a purely external attack by exploitation for instance of a web site to a completely internal attack whereby for instance DBA has accessed data using his normal day-to-day privileges. An attack can be anything between. In my experience, many different types of attacks have happened over many years. For instance, an attacker found out how to request backup tapes from the external store and requested that they are delivered to the company site, whereby he turned up and signed for the tapes. He took them and stole the complete production database. Another example was a person employed as a cleaner where the customers offices were cleaned during the night. The evidence showed that the nefarious database access happened at 2 AM and CCTV confirmed it was a person employed as a cleaner using another employee's PC, which was left turned on and unlocked. In fact, in the organization, every PC was left on 24 hours a day. After this attack, that changed.

Establishing if an attack has occurred can be complex and initially there must be some suspicion and that suspicion must be investigated. It's very difficult in advance to specify rules, unfortunately.

Collecting Artifacts

The main activity of incident response is to collect artifacts from the server, from the database, and from other targets such as web servers. There are two general ways to collect artifacts—the first is scripted and structured and second is ad hoc. Clearly we should plan and obtain a toolkit in advance to assist in extracting artifacts from a database. The incident responder should already be familiar with the tools and know how to install them or use them in a response. The responder should also have tested the tools in advance to know how they behave and what to expect in terms of results. For a live response, a preset list of actions should be defined to extract from the server and the database. Therefore, this extraction can very easily be scripted if necessary.

It makes sense to use pre-defined tools, scripts to extract the data, and then automate the process. Don't discount ad hoc methods to gather additional data if necessary, but ideally have predefined scripts and tools.

An incident responder should not be connected to the target system and describing views or describing tables and trying to develop queries in the system that is being investigated. If that is necessary, then this should be done on a test database. When the query has been completely defined, you then run it on the target system and document it.

Disconnecting the System or Shutting Down

The first reaction if a breach is in progress may be to disconnect the database from the network or shut it down—or worse, pull the power plug. All members of the incident response team and the DBA team must understand *not* to disconnect the database from the network or shut it down.

The incident response team must control these two actions. It is important to understand that the database contains a lot of volatile information that will be lost if the database is powered down abruptly or shut down normally. It may also be the case that an attacker has left code in the database—perhaps as a trigger—so that if it is shut down, it will delete evidence that he left. This could be deleting audit records or removing users or procedures from the database. The biggest loss in shutting a database down immediately would be that the SGA is cleared and all of the transient data is lost. This information is important, as it shows which SQL ran most recently, which users are currently logged in and active, and which processes and sessions are running.

If the attacker is still in the database, he almost certainly is connecting remotely to the database either through a web server or a direct SQL connection. His actions may lead to further loss of data or destruction, but the evidence gained may prove useful in the investigation. A decision needs to be made by the incident response team as to exactly when to disconnect the database from the network and when and if to shut it down.

Clearly, all the volatile evidence must be collected first.

Connecting to the System

To enable collection of artifacts from the database, a connection must be made to the database. Although it could be possible to extract some information from the SGA with a direct connection to the shared memory using a C program, there is no publicly available C program to do this.

You would have to write it yourself. Also if a direct connection to the SGA was used there would be differences to that program based on Oracle version and the operating systems used to support Oracle. This would cause the need to have different programs created for each platform and each version. This is not practical. Also this method would only allow connection to the SGA and would not allow SQL to be executed.

It may be possible to connect to the database using an operating system debugger. Tanel Poder has discuss this on his blog at http://blog. tanelpoder.com/2008/06/14/debugger-dangers/ and http://blog. tanelpoder.com/2013/05/27/debugger-dangers-part-2/, but it's clear that these are very unreliable and unstable methods to access an Oracle database for forensics.

Clearly the access should be using a standard SQL type tool such as SQL*Plus. In fact I recommend using SQL*Plus over graphical tools such as SQL*Developer or TOAD. A command-line tool has a much smaller footprint on the server and therefore is less likely to disturb anything else.

A further question arises as to whether to connect to the database from the server or remotely from a client. Connecting from the server would make sense but there are side issues with this. Accessing the server will change the server because the connection must be made perhaps causing logging or auditing to be written to the server at the operating system level. Also if the investigation is done from the server, then the artifacts arc likely to also be written to the server. Being on the server doesn't mean physically standing next to it; in this context it means making an ssh connection as a Unix user (or Windows user If the platform is Windows) and then accessing the database with SQL*Plus. The simple solution to this is to store the artifacts on removable media, but if the connection is made remotely and no access to the server room is possible, then inserting a USB drive into the server is not likely to be possible. It is probably possible to remotely mount a USB drive, but again this will change the server.

The most sensible approach and the cleanest is to access the database remotely using SQL*Net from a client PC. The incident response practitioner should use a PC prepared for the incident response. Ideally, an encrypted container can be created on the PC using software such as Drivecrypt from a vendor in Germany. The free alternative Truecrypt is no longer supported and available. An encrypted container is a good option, as it allows all tools to be installed into the container or accessed from within the container and all the results to be stored in the container. As soon as the investigation is closed, the container can be locked to prevent access to the data that has been gathered by anyone else.

As part of the investigation, a new user should not be created in the database for the investigator. In other circumstances, such as a security audit, this would be the right thing to do. In the case of forensic analysis, this should not be done as the database should not be changed to add a new user. This would certainly change the SGA and certainly change the data dictionary. Normally it would not be recommended to use the SYS user for security work, as this allows access to do anything. But other than the SYSTEM user, this is the only user guaranteed to exist in any database. Why not use the SYSTEM user? Because in later versions such as 12.2.0.1 some dictionary tables are not accessible to this user. Again, this is for the same reasons we would not want to make grants to this user simply to access objects that are necessary for the investigation. One example is the SYS.USER$ table, which is no longer accessed with the SELECT ANY DICTIONARY system privilege in 12.2.0.1.

It makes sense also to use an Oracle instant client, as it is freely available and much smaller than a complete client. A complete client is usually around 1.2GB, but the instant client is approximately 120MB. This leaves a much smaller footprint.

In summary, use simple tools such as SQL*Plus, use an instant client, connect remotely from a secured PC, and use the SYS user.

Live Response and Artifact Collection

Live response is the process of collecting the evidence from the server and the database. This should be done in a reasonably specific order. Start with the server first and collecting the most volatile evidence so that any change caused by incident collection activities will have the least effect on the rest of the artifacts that you collect. After the most volatile records are collected from the server, then move on to the less volatile and finally the almost static.

At this point, the connection can be made to the Oracle database as discussed in the previous section and artifact collection can begin within the database. Again the same process should be followed. The most volatile data should be collected first to ensure that any further collection does not affect the earlier records. In terms of the database, this is the current SQL that is visible in the SGA. Any SQL that is executed could change the current SQL in the buffers in the SGA; therefore, we must collect this first. Collecting this SQL has to be done with an SQL statement, so it could age out another statement from the buffer.

When you start collecting artifacts, ensure a separate directory has been created to store all of those artifacts. Ideally, encrypt this directory:

```
[root@oel59orablog bin]# mkdir /tmp/client-xxx
```

Also, it is worth ensuring that the date format for the database is set to include seconds. Listing 4-1 shows how to check the current date format.

Listing 4-1. Checking the Current Date Format

```
SQL> select * from sys.nls_session_parameters
  2  where parameter='NLS_DATE_FORMAT';

PARAMETER
--------------------------------------------------

VALUE
--------------------------------------------------
```

```
NLS_DATE_FORMAT
DD-MON-RR
```

```
1 row selected.
```

Actually, testing this will affect the SGA, so it is best not to run this query in the target database. This is available if you need to check what is specified if results do not display the best precision. Listing 4-2 shows how to set the date format to include seconds and the timestamp format to include hundredths of seconds.

Listing 4-2. Setting Date and Timestamp Formats

```
SQL> alter session set nls_date_format='YYYYMMDDHH24MISS';
```

```
Session altered.
```

```
SQL> alter session set nls_timestamp_
format='YYYYMMDDHH24MISSFF';
```

```
Session altered.
```

```
SQL>
```

If this is not set, the date format in any query will lose seconds and hundredths of seconds and of course lose accuracy. Using pure numeric settings means that dates can be subtracted or compared numerically more easily without conversion and language or character set issues are removed.

Views, Base Tables, RAC, and Synonyms?

The analysis of a database for forensic issues involves primarily selecting data from tables or views. The use of views to extract data makes that data richer because of the pre-made views of more complex data.

There is a risk that when analyzing a database that someone could have manipulated the source code of the Oracle database. This is covered in the section on rootkits and elsewhere in this book. The source code of the database includes compiled SQL that forms views. This is normal in a database, but because a view is actually just pre-compiled SQL, someone could change or replace that pre-compiled program. The source code of pre-built PL/SQL procedures could also be manipulated to give incorrect results. For instance, the package DBMS_SQLHASH, which can be used to create checksums of database objects could be modified to output a pre-known hash for certain packages, leading the user to believe that the package is genuine and not modified.

The structure of the data dictionary is also complex in that views can read data from many base tables and other views. These other views can also read data from further base tables and yet more views, ad infinitum.

A sample security view is the view DBA_SYS_PRIVS. The text of this view is shown in Listing 4-3.

Listing 4-3. A Listing from the Database of the View DBA_SYS_PRIVS

```
SQL> set long 1000000
SQL> set pages 0
SQL> select text from dba_views
  2  where view_name='DBA_SYS_PRIVS';
select u.name,spm.name,decode(min(mod(option$,
2)),1,'YES','NO'),
       'NO', 'NO'
from  sys.system_privilege_map spm, sys.sysauth$ sa, user$ u
where sa.grantee#=u.user# and sa.privilege#=spm.privilege
  and bitand(nvl(option$, 0), 4) - 0
group by u.name,spm.name
union all
```

```
/* Commonly granted Privileges */
select u.name,spm.name,decode(min(bitand(option$,
16)),16,'YES','NO'),
       'YES', decode(SYS_CONTEXT('USERENV', 'CON_ID'), 1, 'NO',
       'YES')
from   sys.system_privilege_map spm, sys.sysauth$ sa, user$ u
where sa.grantee#=u.user# and sa.privilege#=spm.privilege
  and bitand(option$,8) = 8
group by u.name,spm.name
union all
/* Federationally granted Privileges */
select u.name,spm.name,decode(min(bitand(option$,
128)),128,'YES','NO'),
       'YES',
       decode(SYS_CONTEXT('USERENV', 'IS_APPLICATION_PDB'),
       'YES', 'YES', 'NO')
from   sys.system_privilege_map spm, sys.sysauth$ sa, user$ u
where sa.grantee#=u.user# and sa.privilege#=spm.privilege
  and bitand(option$,64) = 64
group by u.name,spm.name
```

This view is complex and is actually made up from three SELECT statements joined together to give one complete statement via two UNION ALL clauses. This is made up from local standard rights from 11g and earlier and 12c Common privileges and Federationally granted rights. Each section includes a core SQL against three tables—USER$, SYSAUTH$, and SYSTEM_PRIVILEGE_MAP. The differences between the three sections of the UNION are controlled by the OPTION$ column of SYSAUTH$. To ensure that this view and indeed any other view has not been hacked, you have a number of choices. You can:

- Copy the complete SQL of the view into a script and use it as SQL in a script. This is the best approach, as the SQL in the view is the same but you control it, not the Oracle dictionary.

- Develop simpler SQL on only base tables based on the major joins of the view. The risk is that some rows may be lost in future queries or additional incorrect rows revealed because it is not the same SQL.

- Checksum the views and all child views to verify that they have not been modified and use the original views.

In the case of the dynamic views such as V$SQL, these are also complex and are based on a different model. If you take the view V$SQL, you can see its text in Listing 4-4.

Listing 4-4. The Text for V_$SQL

```
SQL> select text from dba_views
  2  where view_name='V_$SQL';
select "SQL_TEXT","SQL_FULLTEXT","SQL_ID","SHARABLE_
MEM","PERSISTENT_MEM","RUN...
S_ROLLING_INVALID","IS_ROLLING_REFRESH_INVALID" from v$sql
```

Some of the text has been removed to save space as the point of interest is the FROM Clause. This says that V$SQL text selects from v$SQL; what's going on? Well V$SQL is not V$SQL but is in fact V_$SQL. This is because V$SQL is a synonym for V_$SQL. The from V$SQL is because V$sql is a fixed view and the text can be found in V$FIXED_VIEW_DEFINITION. Listing 4-5 shows this for v$sql.

Listing 4-5. Fixed View Definition for v$sql

```
SQL> select * from v$fixed_view_definition
  2  where view_name='V$SQL';
V$SQL
select  SQL_TEXT, SQL_FULLTEXT, SQL_ID,  SHARABLE_MEM,
PERSISTENT_MEM, RUNTI
...
NO_INVALIDATE, IS_ROLLING_INVALID, IS_ROLLING_REFRESH_INVALID
from GV$SQL where
inst_id = USERENV('Instance')
        0
```

Some of the code has been removed to save space. This time v$sql
reads from GV$SQL. This is a normal view and its text in DBA_VIEWS shows
that data is selected from gv$sql for GV_$SQL. When the fixed view
definition is examined for gv$sql, then we finally see that the data is read
from x$kglcursor_child. This is complex and involves multiple layers
of views and synonyms. Synonyms pass SELECT statements on V$SQL and
GV$SQL to V_$SQL and GV_$SQL. Just because these are dynamic views does
not mean that they could not be changed. The synonyms could also be
modified to point at hacker versions of any of these views.

What does GV$ and V$ mean? Well, the V$ views means get data from
the current instance and the GV$ view means get data from all instances.
This comes into play with Oracle RAC. If a RAC database is breached, then
the GV$ views must be used, as you could be connected to one instance of
a three-node RAC cluster and the attacker is connected to another. So his
SQL could be visible in one node and not the others.

So again, as with DBA_SYS_PRIVS, you should use base tables. In this
case, X$ tables. Avoid synonyms and ensure that you use the lowest code
in the stack and access the complete database across all instances. Again
the simplest approach is to put the text of the fixed view GV$SQL against
x$kglcursor_child into your script to avoid views and synonyms.

Spreadsheets

Ideally, make all scripts output record-separated rows of data. Commas are not a good choice, as they can appear in data, so a good option is the vertical bar | as a record separator. The data can then be easily loaded into MS Excel (or similar) so that columns of data can be hidden, rearranged, and of course filtered and sorted. This makes analysis easier.

Server and Database State

The first step in live response is to collect as much detail as possible about the current system state—of both the server and database. This should include establishing what processes are running on the operating system; which users are connected to the operating system; and any network connections that are currently established on the operating system.

Similar action should be performed within the database to establish which processes are running within the database, what jobs are running, which users are connected, and ideally what users are doing (the current SQL that is running), and all recent SQL.

It is also important to establish the system time and its offset if any from real time. Also establish the version of the database and its patch set.

This basic information is useful to understand what vulnerabilities may be possible to exploit. The next step is to collect artifacts from the server and database. Some of these processes are covered with examples in the next section.

Get Server Details

This is now the start of the gathering of artifacts from the servers involved and the database. A suitable directory should be created to store this data. The data collected will be used in Chapter 5 to analyze the breach.

All of the scripts used are available for download from
`http://www.petefinnigan.com/forensics/download.zip`, so download
and use these. Some examples are shown for running scripts to obtain
artifacts, some are shown with simple commands, and some are just listed
to preserve space.

The first step is to get details about the database server. First get the
current date and time:

```
[root@oel1124 ~]# date
Sat Jun  3 20:15:23 BST 2017
```

Find out who is logged in:

```
[root@oel1124 ~]# who
root      :0               2017-06-02 15:42
root      pts/1            2017-06-02 15:42 (:0.0)
root      pts/2            2017-06-03 20:15 (192.168.1.89)
[root@oel1124 ~]#
```

Next get the running processes:

```
[root@oel1124 ~]# ps -ef
UID         PID  PPID  C STIME TTY          TIME CMD
root          1     0  0 Jun02 ?        00:00:02 init [5]
root          2     0  0 Jun02 ?        00:00:00 [kthreadd]
root          3     2  0 Jun02 ?        00:00:02 [ksoftirqd/0]
...
root      19980     1  0 02:41 ?        00:00:00 /usr/bin/
                                                 system-config-network
root      19981 19980  0 02:41 ?        00:00:00 /usr/sbin/
                                                 userhelper -w system-
                                                 config-network
root      19984 19981  0 02:41 ?        00:00:08 /usr/bin/python
                                                 /usr/sbin/system-config-
                                                 network-gui
```

```
root      20336  3362  0 03:00 pts/1  00:00:00 su - oracle
oracle    20337 20336  0 03:00 pts/1  00:00:00 -bash
oracle    23002     1  0 06:00 ?      00:01:48 ora_vkrm_bfora
oracle    27621 20337  0 11:42 pts/1  00:00:00 sqlplus   as sysdba
oracle    27624 27621  0 11:42 ?      00:00:00 oraclebfora
(DESCRIPTION=(LOCAL=YFS)(ADDRESS=(PROTOCOL=beq)))
root      30260     2  0 14:58 ?      00:00:05 [kworker/1:2]
[root@oel1124 ~]#
```

Now get the user accounts from the server and groups:

```
[root@oel1124 ~]# cat /etc/passwd
root:x:0:0:root:/root:/bin/bash
...
oracle:x:502:501::/home/oracle:/bin/bash
orablog:x:503:501::/home/orablog:/bin/bash
[root@oel1124 ~]#
```

and

```
[root@oel1124 ~]# cat /etc/group
root:x:0:root
bin:x:1:root,bin,daemon
...
dba:x:501:orablog
orablog:x:503:
[root@oel1124 ~]#
```

Get the server release and versions:

```
[root@oel1124 ~]# cat /etc/redhat-release
Red Hat Enterprise Linux Server release 5.9 (Tikanga)
 [root@oel1124 ~]# uname -r
2.6.39-300.26.1.el5uek
```

List the open ports:

```
[root@oel1124 ~]# netstat -pln
Active Internet connections (only servers)
Proto Recv-Q Send-Q Local Address    State    PID/Program name
tcp       0      0 0.0.0.0:1521      LISTEN   3570/tnslsnr
tcp       0      0 0.0.0.0:22        LISTEN   2562/sshd
tcp       0      0 127.0.0.1:631     LISTEN   2573/cupsd
tcp       0      0 127.0.0.1:25      LISTEN   2608/sendmail
tcp       0      0 0.0.0.0:702       LISTEN   2216/rpc.statd
tcp       0      0 127.0.0.1:2207    LISTEN   2547/python
tcp       0      0 127.0.0.1:2208    LISTEN   2542/./hpiod
tcp       0      0 0.0.0.0:56717     LISTEN   3646/ora_d000_
                                              bfora
tcp       0      0 0.0.0.0:111       LISTEN   2182/portmap
...
```

You'll need to take other steps, including:

- Locating and saving any operating system audit trails

- Dumping the memory of any running process

- Recursive listing of all files and directories on the server including date and timestamps

- Listing all open files using the Unix command lsof

- Getting copies of any log files

- Getting copies of the .bash_history files

- Establishing if audit is enabled and getting a copy; this is different per operating system

Web Server logs

Now access the two web servers that support the public facing web site and backoffice processing in this example system.

Extract the same server information for the two web servers as was extracted for the database server in the last section. This should include the system time for use in correlation of records from different systems.

Locate the web server access and error logs as well:

```
[root@oel59orablog logs]# ls -ltr
total 1100
-rw-r--r-- 1 root root    6229 Oct 31  2013 php.log
-rw-r--r-- 1 root root       5 Jun  2 16:49 httpd.pid
-rw-r--r-- 1 root root   84135 Jun  3 00:23 error_log
-rw-r--r-- 1 root root 1001300 Jun  3 01:56 access_log
[root@oel59orablog logs]#
```

Copy these to your safe storage in readiness for analysis. Ensure that any archived logs are located and copied to your storage.

Collect Oracle Logs Files from the Server

The Oracle database contains a lot of files that could be useful to database analysis. All of these should be located and copied to the analysis safe storage directory.

The following files should be located and copied:

- The database alert log
- The listener log file
- The SYSDBA audit files
- The database initialization files (init and spfile)

- The database password file that contains the SYSDBA password hashes

- Database trace files

- Redo logs

- Database archive logs if they exist

- SQL*Net logs if any exist

- The database system tablespace data file

- The database control files

Most of these files locations can be found by querying the database to get the locations, but at this point in the investigation we do not want to query the target system and risk changing it. The locations can also found by trail and error from the operating system. The example code shows how to find the alter log:

```
[root@oel1124 u01]# find . -name "*alert*" -print 2>/dev/null
...
./app/oracle/diag/rdbms/bfora/bfora/trace/alert_bfora.log
./app/oracle/diag/rdbms/bfora/bfora/alert
./app/oracle/diag/tnslsnr/oel1124/listener/alert
[root@oel1124 u01]#
```

By default, this also locates the background dump destination, as this is the location of the alert log for the database. Obtain the trace files and the alert log. Locate other trace directories, such as the core dump destination and the user dump destination by using a find command to locate .trc files:

```
[root@oel1124 oracle]# find . -name "*.trc" -print 2>/dev/null
./product/11.2.0/db_1/oel1124.localdomain_bfora/sysman/log/
emagentfetchlet.trc
```

```
./product/11.2.0/db_1/oel1124.localdomain_bfora/sysman/log/
emagent_perl.trc
./product/11.2.0/db_1/oel1124.localdomain_bfora/sysman/log/
emoms.trc
./product/11.2.0/db_1/oel1124.localdomain_bfora/sysman/log/
emagent.trc
./product/11.2.0/db_1/oel1124.localdomain_bfora/sysman/log/
emdctl.trc
./diag/rdbms/bfora/bfora/trace/bfora_diag_3602.trc
./diag/rdbms/bfora/bfora/trace/bfora_vkrm_28444.trc
./diag/rdbms/bfora/bfora/trace/bfora_j001_26463.trc
./diag/rdbms/bfora/bfora/trace/bfora_smon_28697.trc
./diag/rdbms/bfora/bfora/trace/bfora_dbrm_3606.trc
./diag/rdbms/bfora/bfora/trace/cdmp_20170503205638/bfora_
m000_22354_bucket.trc
...
./diag/rdbms/bfora/bfora/incident/incdir_8625/bfora_m000_13772_
i8625.trc
./diag/rdbms/bfora/bfora/incident/incdir_9910/bfora_m000_25357_
i9910.trc
[root@oel1124 oracle]#
```

Obtain all of these files for reference and use. The listener log, listener.ora, and sqlnet.ora can be located by running the listener control utility. This is shown in Chapter 2. These files should be obtained and copied to the safe storage.

The initialization and password files are usually in the $ORACLE_HOME/ dbs directory on Unix. So get these files and save them:

```
[root@oel1124 dbs]# ls -al
total 28
drwxr-xr-x  2 oracle dba 4096 Jun  2 15:53 .
drwxrwxr-x 73 oracle dba 4096 Apr  4  2016 ..
```

```
-rw-rw----  1 oracle dba 1544 Jun  2 15:53 hc_bfora.dat
-rw-r--r--  1 oracle dba 2851 May 15  2009 init.ora
-rw-r-----  1 oracle dba   24 Apr  4  2016 lkBFORA
-rw-r-----  1 oracle dba 1536 Apr 12  2016 orapwbfora
-rw-r-----  1 oracle dba 2560 Jun  3 22:05 spfilebfora.ora
[root@oel1124 dbs]# cp orapwbfora /tmp/forensic/
[root@oel1124 dbs]# cp spfilebfora.ora /tmp/forensic/
[root@oel1124 dbs]# cp init.ora /tmp/forensic/
```

Obtain the system tablespace data file and keep a copy in case it's needed for deleted file analysis:

```
[root@oel1124 bfora]# pwd
/u01/app/oracle/oradata/bfora
[root@oel1124 bfora]# cp system01.dbf /tmp/forensic/
```

Obtain all of the other files listed here and ensure that you have copies for the investigation. Some files cannot be found without access to the database. These will include:

- Locations of libraries (DLL or shared objects) used in the database.

- Locations of files accessible from the database using the parameter utl_file_dir (this parameter is deprecated from Oracle 12.2.0.1) and DIRECTORY objects.

- The location of the ASM data files if ASM is used.

- The location of Flashback files if flashback is used.

- The location of files written to the operating system by Java stored in the database.

All of these can be located after the database artifacts are collected and the files are obtained for analysis.

Get Last SQL

The most important first step in collecting artifacts from the database itself is to get the last SQL executed from the SGA. There are a limited number of rows available in the SGA, but if the investigation is started quickly enough then it may be possible to locate SQL statements that are part of the attack.

Tuning tools such as the Oracle tuning and diagnostic pack and statspack or commercial tools such as Quest may also have tables that contain historic SQL.

Connect to the database and set the date format and timestamp format. Then extract the last SQL from the GV$SQL view:

```
SQL> connect sys/oracle1@//192.168.1.85:1521/bfora.localdomain
as sysdba
Connected.
SQL> alter session set nls_date_format='YYYYMMDDHH24MISS';

Session altered.

SQL> alter session set nls_timestamp_
format='YYYYMMDDHH24MISSFF';

Session altered.

SQL>
```

Collect the SQL:

```
SQL> spool sga.lis
SQL> @sga
...
av6t2u4kxhdm1|SELECT * FROM (SELECT a.*, rownum RN FROM
( SELECT * FROM wp_posts  WHERE 1=1  AND (((post_title LIKE
'%x%'))))a)/**/union/**/select/**/33,1,to_timestamp('27-OCT-
13'),to_timestamp('27-OCT-13'),object_name,'x',0,null,'publish',
```

```
'open','open',null,'name',null,null,to_timestamp('27-OCT-
13'),to_timestamp('27-OCT-13'),null,0,null,0,null,null,0,6/**/
from/**/user_objects/**/where/**/object_type/**/in('PACKAGE','
PROCEDURE','FUNCTION','PACKAGE/**/BODY')--%') OR (post_content
LIKE '%x%'))))a)/**/union/**/select/**/33,1,to_timestamp('27-
OCT-13'),to_timestamp('27-OCT-13'),object_name,'x',0,null,
'publish','open','open',null,'name',null,null,to_timestamp
('27-OCT-13'),to_timestamp('27-OCT-13'),null,0,null,0,null,
null,0,6/**/from/**/user_objects/**/where/**/object_type/**/in
('PACKAGE','PROCEDURE','FUNCTION','PACKAGE/**/BODY')--%')) OR
(post_title LIKE '%x%'))))a)/**/union/**/select/**/33,1,
to_timestamp('27-OCT-13'),to_timestamp('27-OCT-13'),object_name,
'x',0,null,'publish','open','open',null,'name',nul|2017-
06-03/02:56:19|90|90|bfora.localdomain|httpd@oel59orablog.
localdomain (TNS V1-V3)||2017-06-03/02:56:19|20170603025618
...

2258 rows selected.

SQL> spool off
```

The SQL here looks like SQL Injection!

Volatile Artifacts

Next, collect other volatile artifacts from the SGA, including sessions and processes that are current in the SGA. The following gets the session details:

```
SQL> spool session.lis
SQL> @session
1|1||0|0|SYS|oracle|3584|oel1124.localdomain|0|UNKNOWN|oracle@
oel1124.localdomain (PMON)|BACKGROUND||||20170602155350|||SYS$B
ACKGROUND
```

...
145|95|ORABLOG|200168|3|ORABLOG|apache|3643|oel59orab
log.localdomain|46266||httpd@oel59orablog.localdomain
(TNS V1-V3)|USER|httpd@oel59orablog.localdomain (TNS V1-
V3)|||20170603011635|||bfora.localdomain
36 rows selected.

SQL> spool off

Do the same with the process details in v$process and the active session history and save the results to safe storage for later analysis.

Database Artifacts

The core database artifacts can now be obtained and saved for later analysis. Most of these can be extracted with scripts available for download from my web site. A number of these will be shown as examples here and then the rest of the sources are listed for you to obtain the data during your own analysis:

First, get the database system date and time:

```
SQL> select sysdate from dual;
20170603231336

SQL>
```

The date is the 3rd June 2017 at a time of 21:13 and 36 seconds. Now get the database version and any patches installed:

```
SQL> select banner from v$version;
Oracle Database 11g Release 11.2.0.4.0 - 64bit Production
PL/SQL Release 11.2.0.4.0 - Production
CORE    11.2.0.4.0      Production
TNS for Linux: Version 11.2.0.4.0 - Production
NLSRTL Version 11.2.0.4.0 - Production

SQL>
```

And the patches:

```
SQL> set serveroutput on
SQL> @print 'select * from dba_registry_history'
old  33:        lv_str:=translate('&&1','''','''''');
new  33:        lv_str:=translate('select * from dba_registry_
                history','''','''''');
Executing Query [select * from dba_registry_history]
ACTION_TIME                  : 20130824120345119862
ACTION                       : APPLY
NAMESPACE                    : SERVER
VERSION                      : 11.2.0.4
ID                           : 0
BUNDLE_SERIES                : PSU
COMMENTS                     : Patchset 11.2.0.2.0
------------------------------------------------
ACTION_TIME                  : 20160404073803616634
ACTION                       : APPLY
NAMESPACE                    : SERVER
VERSION                      : 11.2.0.4
ID                           : 0
BUNDLE_SERIES                : PSU
COMMENTS                     : Patchset 11.2.0.2.0
------------------------------------------------

PL/SQL procedure successfully completed.

SQL>
```

Also obtain the database name, ID, and created date:

```
SQL> select dbid,name,created from v$database;
1487954385 BFORA     20160404073649

SQL>
```

Establish if any audit trails exist in the database and which settings are enabled. To do this, you can run the audit.sql tool, which analyzes audit trail settings:

```
SQL> @audit
...
Core Database Audit     [DB]
SYSDBA Audit            [FALSE]
Audit Trace Location    [/u01/app/oracle/admin/bfora/adump]
Privilege Audit         [144]
Statement Audit         [116]
Object Audit            [89]
...
```

As you can see, this database has a rich audit trail enabled, so we can grab the contents of the AUD$ audit trail:

```
SQL> spool dump_aud.lis
SQL> @dump_aud.sql
...
```

There is also a non-standard audit trail in this database. Actually, it is the PFCLATK audit trail toolkit discussed in Chapter 6. This has some 50,000 records in it:

```
SQL> select count(*) from atkd.pfclatk_audit;
    50923
SQL>
```

The contents of this audit trail also should be extracted from the database and kept for analysis. Now get a list of users:

```
SQL> @user_dump.sql
0,SYS,20130824113740,20160412160636,20130824120704,20130824120704
1,PUBLIC,20130824113740,,,
```

```
2,CONNECT,20130824113740,,,
3,RESOURCE,20130824113740,,,
...

154 rows selected.

SQL> spool off
```

Now dump the library cache:

```
SQL> spool object_cache2.lis
SQL> @db_object_cache
...
^SELECT * FROM (SELECT a.*, rownum RN FROM ( SELECT * FROM
wp_posts  WHERE 1=1  AND (((post_title LIKE '%oracle%')
OR (post_content LIKE '%oracle%')) AND ((post_title LIKE
'%UNION%') OR (post_content LIKE '%UNION%')) AND ((post_
title LIKE '%ALL%') OR (post_content LIKE '%ALL%')) AND
((post_title LIKE '%SELECT%') OR (post_content LIKE
'%SELECT%')) AND ((post_title LIKE '%NULL,NULL,NULL,NULL,NU
LL,NULL%') OR (post_content LIKE '%NULL,NULL,NULL,NULL,NUL
L,NULL%')) AND ((post_title LIKE '%FROM%') OR (post_content
LIKE '%FROM%')) AND ((post_title LIKE '%DUAL--%') OR (post_
content LIKE '%DUAL--%')) AND ((post_title LIKE '%xuEE%') OR
(post_content LIKE '%xuEE%')) OR (post_title LIKE '%oracle
UNION ALL SELECT NULL,NULL,NULL,NULL,NULL,NULL FROM DUAL-
- xuEE%') OR (post_content LIKE '%oracle UNION ALL SELECT
NULL,NULL,NULL,NULL,NULL,NULL FROM DUAL-- xuEE%')) AND post_
date_gmt <= SYSDATE AND (post_status = 'publish') AND post_
status != 'attachment' ORDER BY post_date DESC ) a WHERE rownum
<= 10) WHE
R^^SQL AREA^CURSOR^5696^2^1^1^0^NO^117386^0^2655505034^NULL^NON
E^VALID^2017-06-03/01:36:20^^1^1
```

```
^SELECT * FROM wp_users WHERE user_login = 'x' union
select 1, 'x', run_sql('execute immediate ''alter user
orablog identified by password'';'), 'x', 'x', 'x',to_
timestamp('29-NOV-2013'), 'x',1, 'x' from dual--'^^SQL
AREA^CURSOR^4528^1^2^1^0^NO^0^0^4193683362^NULL^NONE^VALID^
2017-06-03/03:00:47^^1^3
...
```

This sample from the library cache dump shows that SQL Injection was attempted by the attacker—presumably trying to attack a web page and attempting to change the ORABLOG user's password. Now run the jd* scripts to locate all privileges for all users, all members of all roles, all privileges granted to all roles, and all grants to all objects. This can be done by running the following:

- jd_f.sql to get all privileges for all users

- jd_r.sql to get all privileges granted to all roles

- jd_who_has_role.sql to get all role memberships

- jd_obj.sql to get all object grants

Now go ahead and extract all of the other data from the database that may be used in an investigation. This includes:

- All database parameters, including hidden ones.

- All of the database password hashes so that they can be cracked to occ if passwords are very weak.

- A list of all directory objects and the utl_file_dir database parameter to locate all file systems that can be accessed from the database. Check these file systems and list the files to see if any may have been created by the attacker.

- A list of all database links and the databases they connect to and credentials involved.

- A list of all database jobs, scheduler jobs, and the job logs, payloads of jobs, and programs used in jobs.

- List of all database libraries installed.

- List of all users age and profiles using the `age.sql` and `profiles.sql` scripts. This will show protections on users credentials and whether passwords have been changed.

- A list of users including dates and IDs so that an analysis can be made to see if any users have been added and dropped during the attack.

- A list of all objects and assess whether any objects have been created, changed, or dropped.

- Changes to DML from the `MON_MODS$`, `MON_MODS_ALL$`, and `DBA_TAB_MODIFICATIONS` views to see DML changes to tables.

- The contents of the recycle bin.

- A list of all external tables.

- The contents of the `COL_USAGE$` table to assess if any tables have been included in a where clause.

- All source code for Java, PL/SQL, triggers, and types.

- Check which triggers and their types are enabled.

Checksums

To establish the integrity of the database, it is necessary to create checksums of the database objects to include:

- All PL/SQL source code

- Source code of views

- Source code of triggers

- Table structures

- All Java code in the database

The checksums should be generated and stored externally so that checksums can also be generated on a "good" known system and compared with those generated on the target database. This comparison can be used to validate any object in the target database.

Do not generate and store the hashes in the target system, even for copying out to somewhere else. This would make changes to the target system, which would invalidate it. Also, while these checksums are stored in the target, the attacker (if still present) could change them.

A sample checksum is here:

```
SQL> @checksum
HR|ADD_JOB_HISTORY|PROCEDURE|AE9EA3261E7626A30AED8131BB3E57E8FA
72A1AE
HR|SECURE_DML|PROCEDURE|476E086F11DDAC477827654F3B91F9AF3D84C47E
HR|SECURE_EMPLOYEES|TRIGGER|8EF93443488D1B45832A909AED81DAAC9E1FCA6E
HR|UPDATE_JOB_HISTORY|TRIGGER|B03EF89E7849E38BB97AD1867405ED240
CBC7ED4

...
```

CHAPTER 5

Forensic Analysis

This chapter focuses on the forensic analysis process by using a simple example of a compromised system. The attacker has managed to exploit the database through a web-based application and we going to use some of the lessons from Chapter 2 around artifact collection and from Chapter 3 using the structure of an incident response process. The attack of our sample system was introduced in Chapter 4.

The pre-analysis section discusses what should be done first; initially, take a step back to plan and make sure nothing is rushed. An Oracle database is a very complex system and it needs to be carefully analyzed and dealt with. Example analysis will then be walked through using the data that has been collected from the attack in Chapter 4 to show how each of the artifacts fit together to prove that an attack has taken place and from where, as well as how and when the attacker get in and stole the data.

In the post analysis section, basic questions will be answered such as how the attacker got in, what rights did he have while he was in the database, what did he see while he was in the database, what did he change while he was in the database if anything, and—importantly—what could he have done if he had more Oracle based skills.

Chapter 5 concludes with a discussion of the findings and assumptions of the sample analysis and briefly discusses creating a report and summary that can be presented to relevant business managers or even authorities. Finally, a discussion around whether to restore and rebuild the database is made.

© Pete Finnigan 2018
P. Finnigan, *Oracle Incident Response and Forensics*,
https://doi.org/10.1007/978-1-4842-3264-4_5

Pre-Analysis

This chapter focuses on the forensic analysis of the same attack that we started in Chapter 4. Before a detailed analysis of a target system can take place, we must collect all the required artifacts from:

- The target database server—the server that hosts the database

- The database itself

- The web servers

- Other targets as necessary

The data that was collected must be stored and used in a trusted and secure way in accordance with the chain of custody rules. The integrity of the data must also be established and checked. This is normally by checksumming the data collected and the database structure to prove whether the attacker has changed it. Checksumming helps prove collected data has not been modified by the collection and analysis process. Checksumming also helps with the restoration of the database and its application process. If you can prove that the basic structure of the database is intact and has not been changed by the attacker, there is less risk in not doing a full restore.

The analysis presented in this chapter is of course related to the sample application and the attack against it. This is specific to this database and this application but the ideas and techniques presented here should help in any forensic investigation.

Example Analysis

In the section, we are going to look at a sample analysis of a potential breach of a sample database running two applications. The simulated attack was described briefly in Chapter 4 before we looked at the artifact collection process in the live response. Chapters 4 and 5 focus on the simple example of an attack; Chapter 4 looks at the data collection and Chapter 5 looks at the analysis after the data collection.

The forensic analysis should first establish if the breach has indeed occurred. As discussed earlier, there is no hard and set rule to do this. Establishing if a breach occurred depends on a lot of factors. The simplest is that it has become publicly known that business-critical data has become available in a non-standard way. If data has not been exposed publicly, it becomes harder to establish that a breach has occurred; perhaps someone has reported an employee for having access to systems they should not have. Maybe a cleaner was seen at 2AM logging in to a DBA workstation or maybe a lady who works in customer support was seen accessing the HR system by another employee. Another example for establishing that a breach has actually occurred could be that an audit trail created an alert that showed that someone was making grants or creating users in the database outside of normal change control.

The possibilities for establishing that a breach has occurred need investigation and knowledge of the business and IT infrastructure specific to the system in question. This is always going to be difficult to establish in advance, as there are no set rules to do this. It takes detective-like investigation.

For this forensic analysis example, the sample company system that we described is aware of credit card details and personally identifiable information being posted to the Facebook web site and some records being exposed on Twitter. Figure 5-1 shows a post made by the attacker of some credit card details to the Facebook web site.

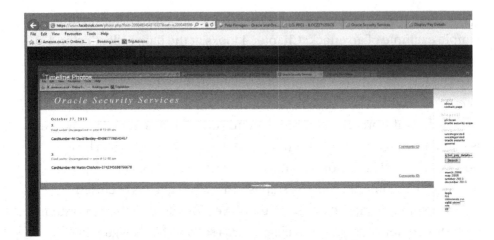

Figure 5-1. *The customer's credit card data is leaked to Facebook. Copyright (c) PeteFinnigan.com Limited. Used with permission.*

Remember that there is a video detailing the actual attack that is the focus of this chapter. You can view this video after reading this chapter; the link is provided at the end.

Often with a web-based attack, there can be lots of preparatory hacks done by the attacker. This may be manually done or could use automated SQL Injection tools. In researching an attack, we need to establish whether the attack was manual or tool driven. If it was tool driven, it's likely that the attacker had little skill; i.e., he just downloaded the tool from the Internet and pointed it at your web site. If the attack was manual, it's more likely that it was a skilled attacker and therefore you should be more aware of trying to establish exactly what he did. Trying to assess if an attack used tools or not is difficult. As with anything, the evidence depends on what was caught and the tools that were used.

This post to Facebook is the starting point of this investigation; we know that sensitive data has been exposed so our incident response process must be triggered.

The first step is to establish if the data posted to the Internet was genuine. This phase of the investigation will require ad hoc queries because we need to find the data in the database. This cannot be preplanned and scripted. Here is a search looking for any database table that might include credit card details:

```
SQL> select owner,table_name from dba_tables
  2  where table_name like '%CREDIT%';
ORABLOG           CREDIT_CARDS_DEV
ORABLOG           CREDITCARD
ORABLOG           CREDIT_CARD
```

Is one of these tables the source of the leak? The first step is to describe each table and see if it includes columns that store credit card details and names.

```
SQL> desc orablog.credit_card
 Name                    Null?     Type
 ------------------      --------  --------------
 NAME_ON_CARD                      VARCHAR2(100)
 FIRST_NAME                        VARCHAR2(50)
 LAST_NAME                         VARCHAR2(50)
 PAN                               RAW(100)

SQL> desc orablog.creditcard
 Name                    Null?     Type
 ------------------      --------  --------------
 NAME_ON_CARD                      VARCHAR2(100)
 FIRST_NAME                        VARCHAR2(50)
 LAST_NAME                         VARCHAR2(50)
 PAN                               RAW(100)
```

```
SQL> desc orablog.credit_cards_dev
 Name                    Null?    Type
 -------------------     -------- --------------
 NAME_ON_CARD                     VARCHAR2(100)
 FIRST_NAME                       VARCHAR2(50)
 LAST_NAME                        VARCHAR2(50)
 CARD_NUMBER                      VARCHAR2(4000)
```

Clearly all of these tables could have provided the data that the attacker displayed. We know the surnames of the two records shown, so we can search in each of these tables to see if this exists. None of these tables holds this data, so they are clearly not the source of the leak.

We can also establish at this stage the likely attack vector used by the hacker. Clearly, there is a clue in the screenshot that he took. The screenshot is of the public facing web site and careful analysis shows part of what looks like SQL in the search box. The piece we can see says g.bof_pay_details--.

A description of this table is:

```
SQL> desc orablog.bof_pay_details
 Name                    Null?       Type
 -------------------     --------    --------------
 ID                      NOT NULL    NUMBER
 PAYMENT_ID              NOT NULL    NUMBER
 NAME_ON_CARD            NOT NULL    VARCHAR2(100)
 CC34                    NOT NULL    RAW(100)
 START_DATE                          DATE
 END_DATE                NOT NULL    DATE
 LAST_FOUR               NOT NULL    VARCHAR2(4)
```

```
SQL>
```

A quick check of the contents of this table proves that this is the source of the leak. This can be seen here:

```
SQL> select name_on_card,cc34
  2  from orablog.bof_pay_details;
Mr David Bentley
C795C9199A78988F3D375D5297AED40342AAF4A32FE28A2D

Mr Martin Chisholm
E634E4CF55C484B4E8924F5CF3C79D29D68ACDD2FC06F8BC

2 rows selected.


SQL>
```

The number of records match and the names are exactly the same, so in this case, this probably proves the data came from this database and this table. The owner of the table is ORABLOG and this is also the same user who connected the webserver to the database. This is likely to be part of the reason the attack succeeded.

This proves the attack is real; we also know how the attacker got in at this point. He entered the database by SQL Injecting the company's public web site. It is worth checking if there is a difference between the timestamps on the web server, the database server, and the database:

```
[root@oel59orablog client-xxx]# date
Sun Jun  4 06:24:32 BST 2017
[root@oel59orablog client-xxx]# ssh root@192.168.1.85
root@192.168.1.85's password:
Last login: Sun Jun  4 01:56:31 2017 from 192.168.1.89
[root@oel1124 ~]# date
Sun Jun  4 01:59:56 BST 2017
[root@oel1124 ~]# exit
logout
```

```
Connection to 192.168.1.85 closed.
[root@oel59orablog client-xxx]# ./env

SQL*Plus: Release 12.1.0.1.0 Production on Sun Jun 4 06:24:58 2017

Copyright (c) 1982, 2013, Oracle.  All rights reserved.

SQL> connect sys/oracle1@//192.168.1.85:1521/bfora.localdomain
as sysdba
Connected.
SQL> alter session set nls_date_format='DD-MON-YYYY
HH24:MI:SS';

Session altered.


SQL> select sysdate from dual;

SYSDATE
--------------------
04-JUN-2017 02:00:48

SQL>
```

There is a big discrepancy between these dates. All have dates on 4
June 2017, but the times are different. The web server shows 06:24, the
database server shows 01:59, and the database shows 02:00. The database
in the database server is likely to be on the exact same timestamp if the
difference is due to the time taken to type in the commands. The web
server and database differ by four hours and 20 minutes. This must be
taken into account when comparing records.

A review of the web server error log does not help with the analysis of
this attack. There are very few records for 2017 and none of them stand out
as potential SQL Injection.

Next, look at the access log for the web server. A search of the access log looking for the database table BOF_PAY_DETAILS shows just two entries in 2017:

```
192.168.1.56 - - [03/Jun/2017:01:53:02 +0100] "GET /index.php?s
=x%25%27%29%29%29%29a%29%2F**%2Funion%2F**%2Fselect%2F**%2F33%2
C1%2Cto_timestamp%28%2727-OCT-13%27%29%2Cto_timestamp%28%2727-
OCT-13%27%29%2C%27CardNumber-%27%7C%7Cname_on_card%7C%7C%27-
%27%7C%7Cbof_kkrc.dr%28cc34%29%2C%27x%27%2C0%2Cnull%2C%27publis
h%27%2C%27open%27%2C%27open%27%2Cnull%2C%27name%27%2Cnull%2Cnu
ll%2Cto_timestamp%28%2727-OCT-13%27%29%2Cto_timestamp%28%2727-
OCT-13%27%29%2Cnull%2C0%2Cnull%2C0%2Cnull%2Cnull%2C0%2C6%2F**%2
Ffrom%2F**%2Forablog.bof_pay_details-- HTTP/1.1" 200 5367
192.168.1.56 - - [03/Jun/2017:01:56:19 +0100] "GET /index.php?s
=x%25%27%29%29%29%29a%29%2F**%2Funion%2F**%2Fselect%2F**%2F33%2
C1%2Cto_timestamp%28%2727-OCT-13%27%29%2Cto_timestamp%28%2727-
OCT-13%27%29%2C%27CardNumber-%27%7C%7Cname_on_card%7C%7C%27-
%27%7C%7Cbof_kkrc.dr%28cc34%29%2C%27x%27%2C0%2Cnull%2C%27publis
h%27%2C%27open%27%2C%27open%27%2Cnull%2C%27name%27%2Cnull%2Cnu
ll%2Cto_timestamp%28%2727-OCT-13%27%29%2Cto timestamp%28%2727-
OCT-13%27%29%2Cnull%2C0%2Cnull%2C0%2Cnull%2Cnull%2C0%2C6%2F**%2
Ffrom%2F**%2Forablog.bof_pay_details-- HTTP/1.1" 200 5367
```

These are clearly SQL Injection. The dates also show that the attack took place on 3 June 2017 at 01:53. As this time is very late for the UK where the database and web server are located, this may indicate an attacker who is in the United States. The IP address of the attacker is also located as 192.168.1.56. In this example, this IP address is not public and is on the author's private network, but in a real investigation this would give us a clue as to who the attacker may be and we could analyze the IP address or hostname to find out more. This may involve research into ISPs and other details to isolate the attacker. We can now search in the access log to see how many entries the attacker made.

```
[root@oel59orablog logs]# grep 192.168.1.56 access_log | wc -l
1612
[root@oel59orablog logs]#
```

There are a lot of entries, which can indicate a scripted tool-based attack. The first entry for this IP address is:

```
192.168.1.56 - - [02/Jun/2017:16:49:34 +0100] "GET / HTTP/1.1"
200 8314
```

The last is:

```
192.168.1.56 - - [03/Jun/2017:01:56:19 +0100] "GET /index.php?s
=x%25%27%29%29%29%29a%29%2F**%2Funion%2F**%2Fselect%2F**%2F33%2
C1%2Cto_timestamp%28%2727-OCT-13%27%29%2Cto_timestamp%28%2727-
OCT-13%27%29%2C%27CardNumber-%27%7C%7Cname_on_card%7C%7C%27-
%27%7C%7Cbof_kkrc.dr%28cc34%29%2C%27x%27%2C0%2Cnull%2C%27publis
h%27%2C%27open%27%2C%27open%27%2Cnull%2C%27name%27%2Cnull%2Cnu
ll%2Cto_timestamp%28%2727-OCT-13%27%29%2Cto_timestamp%28%2727-
OCT-13%27%29%2Cnull%2C0%2Cnull%2C0%2Cnull%2Cnull%2C0%2C6%2F**%2
Ffrom%2F**%2Forablog.bof_pay_details-- HTTP/1.1" 200 5367
```

This shows that the attack took place between the 2nd June 2017 at 16:49 and the 3rd June 2017 at 01:56 and that the attacker made over 1,600 requests to the database.

This is the same record we saw earlier, so it seems the attacker's goal was to steal credit cards and when he got them he left. Figure 5-2 shows browsing the access_log for more details.

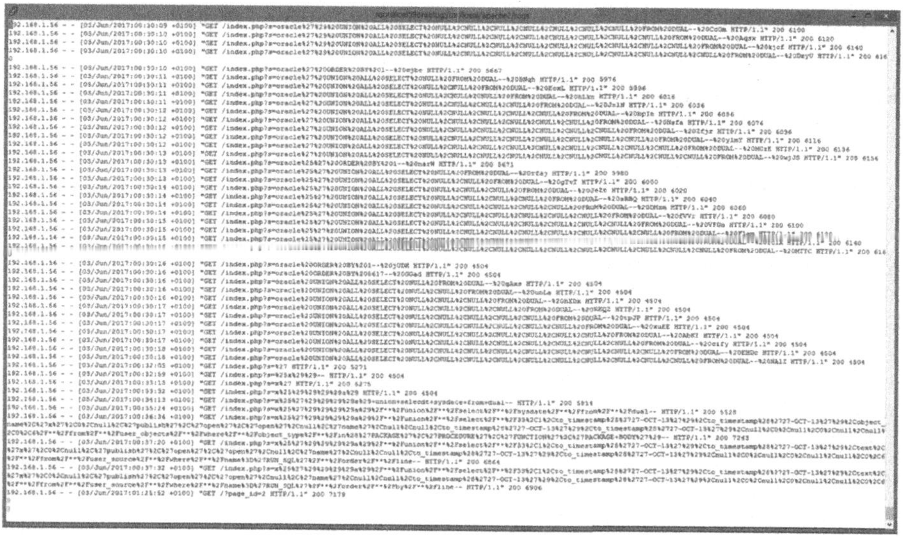

Figure 5-2. *Showing more details in the access_log. Copyright (c) PeteFinnigan.com Limited. Used with permission.*

The analysis of the access log indicates that the attacker made manual attacks and succeeded in reading credit card details. But it also shows that he used an automated tool; this is clear from the log, as requests are extended to add more elements to potential SQL and multiple requests are executed per second. This has to be scripted. The attacks where he gets the credit card details were much slower and were therefore manual. We can assume that he started with a tool and then continued manually once he was convinced that the database was vulnerable. Or, it could have been two people—an initial unskilled person and then a much more skilled second person. We may never know!

Figure 5-3 shows the tool that was possibly used—`sqlmap`.

Figure 5-3. *An example of using sqlmap (c) Copyright PeteFinnigan. com Limited. Used with permission.*

What are the access permissions on the `ORABLOG.BOF_PAY_DETAILS` table? We can get this from our object dump evidence in Chapter 4:

```
Testing root object => [ORABLOG.BOF_PAY_DETAILS]


GRANTOR        GRANTEE         S I U D A F D I R Q C E
-------------  --------------- - - - - - - - - - - - -

PL/SQL procedure successfully completed.
```

This is interesting, as there are no grants on this table. But this is not an issue for the attacker, as he is connected as the schema owner `ORABLOG`. We can see this in the `access_log` with a little perseverance:

```
[root@oel59orablog logs]# grep 192.168.1.56 access_log | grep
user | grep dual
192.168.1.56 - - [03/Jun/2017:01:48:42 +0100] "GET /index.php?s
=x%25%27%29%29%29%29a%29%2F**%2Funion%2F**%2Fselect%2F**%2F33%2
C1%2Cto_timestamp%28%2727-OCT-13%27%29%2Cto_timestamp%28%2727-
OCT-13%27%29%2Cuser%2C%27x%27%2C0%2Cnull%2C%27publish%27%2C
%27open%27%2C%27open%27%2Cnull%2C%27name%27%2Cnull%2Cnull%2C
to_timestamp%28%2727-OCT-13%27%29%2Cto_timestamp%28%2727-OCT-
13%27%29%2Cnull%2C0%2Cnull%2C0%2Cnull%2Cnull%2C0%2C6%2F**%2Ffrom%
2F**%2Fdual-- HTTP/1.1" 200 4887
[root@oel59orablog logs]#
```

So the attacker knew what he was doing and was able to see who he was logged in as. The `access_log` also shows that he viewed a list of database tables, a list of procedures, and the source code of the encryption routine for the credit card processing.

A review of the library cache dump that we took also shows in Figure 5-4 that the attacker used SQL Injection to read the encryption key that is stored in a file called `.key` on the file system as well as the source code of the encryption routine written in PL/SQL.

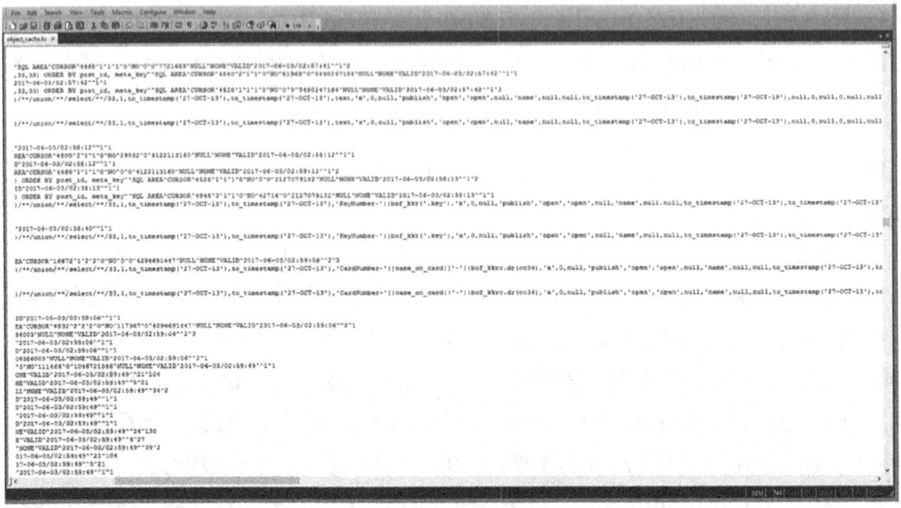

Figure 5-4. *Library cache showing the attacker's actions.*
Copyright (c) PeteFinnigan.com Limited. Used with permission.

Another interesting entry in the library cache shows:

```
^begin execute/**/immediate/**/'noaudit/**/select/**/on/**/
orablog.credit_card'; end;^^SQL AREA^CURSOR^4768^2^1^1^0^NO^111
466^0^1046721386^NULL^NONE^VALID^2017-06-03/02:59:49^^1^1
```

The attacker executed DDL against the database and disabled audit
trail settings on the ORABLOG.CREDIT_CARD table. How did he do this via
SQL Injection:

```
192.168.1.56 - - [03/Jun/2017:01:53:45 +0100] "GET /index.
php?s=x%25%27%29%29%29%29a%29%2F**%2Funion%2F**%2Fselect
%2F**%2F33%2C1%2Cto_timestamp%28%2727-OCT-13%27%29%2Cto_
timestamp%28%2727-OCT-13%27%29%2Crun_sql%28%27execute%2F**%
2Fimmediate%2F**%2F%27%27noaudit%2F**%2Fselect%2F**%2Fon%2F
**%2Forablog.credit_card%27%27%3B%27%29%2C%27x%27%2C0%2Cnul
l%2C%27publish%27%2C%27open%27%2C%27open%27%2Cnull%2C%27nam
e%27%2Cnull%2Cnull%2Cto_timestamp%28%2727-OCT-13%27%29%2Cto_
```

```
timestamp%28%2727-OCT-13%27%29%2Cnull%2C0%2Cnull%2C0%2Cnull%2C
null%2C0%2C6%2F**%2Ffrom%2F**%2Fdual-- HTTP/1.1" 200 4976
```

This shows that he used a procedure called `ORABLOG.RUN_SQL` to execute DDL. He can do this as this procedure allows any code to be run as the owner (ORABLOG), so DDL is allowed and the owner can disable his own audit without audit system privileges.

Another interesting entry in the library cache is:

```
^SELECT * FROM wp_users WHERE user_login = 'x' union select 1,
'x', run_sql('execute immediate ''alter user orablog identified
by password'';'), 'x', 'x', 'x',to_timestamp('29-NOV-2013'),
'x',1, 'x' from dual--'^^SQL AREA^CURSOR^4528^1^2^1^0^NO^0^0^41
93683362^NULL^NONE^VALID^2017-06-03/03:00:47^^1^3
^SELECT * FROM wp_users WHERE user_login = 'x' union select 1,
'x', run_sql('execute immediate ''alter user orablog identified
by password'';'), 'x', 'x', 'x',to_timestamp('29-NOV-2013'),
'x',1, 'x' from dual--'^^SQL AREA^CURSOR^4896^2^2^1^0^NO^34722^
0^4193683362^NULL^NONE^VALID^2017-06-03/03:00:47^^1^1
```

This shows that he changed the ORABLOG password again using the same procedure RUN_SQL, which allows DDL, but this time via a different vector as the URL is much simpler. This is in fact the logon dialog of the web site and the SQL is sent twice because there is a password field and a username field.

Are there any audit trail records that tell us anything? As a matter of fact, the detailed audit in the database captured most of the attacker's actions; in particular, the DDL that disabled the audit and changed the password.

The user dump taken from the database for the ORABLOG user shows:

```
90,ORABL
OG,20160404143947,20170603030158,20170427190058,20160404143947
```

This confirms from the PTIME date on the user's table that the password was changed. No other user passwords were changed in the short period between the 2nd June and the 3rd June 2017. ID analysis shows that no user was added:

```
259,ATKR,20170426160152,20170426160152,,
262,DEV,20170426173649,20170426173649,,
263,_NEXT_USER,20130824113740,,,
```

The last user ID, 262, was added April 2017 and the next user is 263, so no user was dropped; otherwise, it would be higher than 263. So we know the attacker did not create any users or change any other passwords.

A review of the object dump again as with users gives us reasonable confidence that no database objects were added and/or dropped. This means that we probably do not need to analyze the redo logs or look for deleted data in the system tablespace data file.

The listener log gives little new detail, as we have learned a lot from the other logs.

The hacker used ORABLOG and its permissions from the jd_f.sql script results are:

```
User => ORABLOG has been granted the following privileges
================================================================
          ROLE => CONNECT which contains =>
            SYS PRIV => CREATE SESSION grantable => NO
          ROLE => RESOURCE which contains =>
            SYS PRIV => CREATE CLUSTER grantable => NO
            SYS PRIV => CREATE INDEXTYPE grantable => NO
            SYS PRIV => CREATE OPERATOR grantable => NO
            SYS PRIV => CREATE PROCEDURE grantable => NO
            SYS PRIV => CREATE SEQUENCE grantable => NO
```

```
SYS PRIV => CREATE TABLE grantable => NO
SYS PRIV => CREATE TRIGGER grantable => NO
SYS PRIV => CREATE TYPE grantable => NO
SYS PRIV => CREATE ANY CONTEXT grantable => NO
SYS PRIV => CREATE PROCEDURE grantable => NO
SYS PRIV => CREATE VIEW grantable => NO
SYS PRIV => UNLIMITED TABLESPACE grantable => NO
TABLE PRIV => EXECUTE object => FACADM.Count[1] grantable
=> NO
TABLE PRIV => EXECUTE object => SEED.Count[1] grantable
=> NO
TABLE PRIV => EXECUTE object => SYS.Count[3] grantable =>
NO
TABLE PRIV => READ object => SYS.Count[1] grantable => NO
TABLE PRIV => SELECT object => IMPORTER.Count[1]
grantable => NO
TABLE PRIV => WRITE object => SYS.Count[1] grantable => NO
```

PL/SQL procedure successfully completed.

The permissions allow the attacker to do anything to the existing ORABLOG objects and create new ones but little else. He could exploit an unfixed bug in the database, as the database has not had a CPU applied since the release of Oracle 11.2.0.4, but there is no evidence of a direct connection to the database as ORABLOG or any other user, and there is no evidence of using or accessing Oracle packages via the web logs or the audit or library cache.

Post-Analysis

We learned a lot about the attackers actions in the database from a few collected resources and we can correlate these with other resources that we took from the target database and web server.

It is now important for this analysis to revisit our simple questions again and see if we can answer them succinctly.

How Did He Get In?

The attacker accessed the database via a vulnerable web application from the company's public web site using SQL Injection through the web site's search box and via the web site's admin logon form.

It is unlikely that he gained access to the database by other means. It is also unlikely that he accessed other databases, as this database has no links.

He did access the file system indirectly by reading the encryption key via SQL Injection.

What Rights Did He Have?

The attacker had the rights of the ORABLOG user, who owns the schema for the public web site and the back office application. While he could manipulate the application's functions and data, he could not access other schemas without considerably more skill to locate weaknesses.

What Did He See?

He read the credit card details, including the payment card numbers, personal details, user lists for the database, credit card encryption codes, and lists of all tables and PL/SQL code in the database as well as the encryption key.

What Did He Change?

He was able to disable audit on the credit card table and change the ORABLOG user's password. This would have been noticed as soon as the current logged-in sessions from the web server were closed.

What Could He Have Done?

He could have stolen all customer data and code and database structure for the application. With some skill, he maybe could have found a general vulnerability in Oracle code, but there is no evidence that he did.

He seems skilled and his target was customer data, which he got. He also seems to have left as soon as he achieved his goal and he also displayed some levels of skill.

Findings

The database design and application have weaknesses:

- The two applications share a schema

- The two applications log in as the schema

- There are SQL Injection issues in the application code

- The encryption code is reasonable but its weakness is that it is in the same schema

- The audit trail was good

Some high-level solutions could be:

- Split frontoffice and backoffice applications into separate schema

- Move security code such as encryption to separate schemas

- Do not allow the applications to connect as the schema owners

- Fix the SQL Injection

All of this would prevent these hacks. SQL Injection could not be used to access backoffice data or code or decrypt cards. The current design is lazy, as it means no privileges are needed between the connected user and the data and code. This of course means that an attacker has an advantage in this case.

As part of the solution to solve the problems highlighted by this attack, we need to remove the duplicate credit card tables from the database identified earlier.

Report and Summary

A detailed report should be created that presents the analysis in a logical manner, as we have done in this chapter. The report should focus on the key issues and questions that we discussed in the last section. The summary should answer those questions but, as in the last section, it should focus on what's broken in the database security and what are the best ways to fix this.

Clearly, the report could also be intended for law enforcement and therefore should contain chain of custody information and documentation to prove the integrity of the data gathered and tools used.

Restore and Rebuild

Should the database be destroyed and rebuilt or can it be repaired? This all depends on the particular breach of course. In the example we presented in this book, it's clear that the attacker stole data and changed audit settings and passwords.

In this case, we almost certainly do not need to rebuild and business can continue without a break or need to reload data manually. We do need to change the design, as discussed, and add better security—this issue is discussed in Chapter 6.

In other cases, if data is stolen but no evidence of change is found, it's possible not to rebuild. If changes are found or the full extent of the attacker activities is not known, it's better to rebuild but still fix the security layers in the database.

CHAPTER 6

What To Do Next?

Be realistic, most Oracle databases are not super locked down, and you cannot always trust all your staff, even those who have elevated credentials, to access the database. Therefore you have to assume it's a matter of *if* not *when* you will be attacked. This means you must be prepared. You must know how to understand if you've been breached and you must know how to respond to an incident. Clearly, forensic analysis to understand how the attack played out is very important and must be understood in advance, even if you don't do the analysis yourself.

Preparing to be attacked does not mean that you want to be attacked; it just means you accept in advance that it is a possibility. Adding security and lockdown to your Oracle database costs money, but it may cost you even more money when you're actually breached. A simpler first step is to include a very useful and comprehensive audit trail that would detect an attack. In this way, you would be able to react much more instantaneously and potentially even stop the removal of data that an attacker would like to steal. Having a comprehensive audit trail will also aid the analysis process and help you understand exactly what happened.

Planning

Planning is the most important step of the incident response process. If you do not have a plan, you simply don't know what to do when an attack occurs. Planning involves a number of elements. The steps that should be

© Pete Finnigan 2018
P. Finnigan, *Oracle Incident Response and Forensics*,
https://doi.org/10.1007/978-1-4842-3264-4_6

followed when an incident occurs should be prepared and documented in advance. This should be signed off on and all relevant members of staff should be trained to understand what should happen when an incident occurs.

This plan does not need to be complex; in fact, a reasonable plan can fit on a single sheet of paper. The plan should include how to report and handle the raising of an incident; it should include who the leader of the response to the incident is and it should identify a team and the tools that they will use to investigate and analyze the incident.

With new regulations, such as GDPR, coming into force in early 2018 in the UK and the EU, it is more important than ever, at least on that side of the Atlantic, that a business knows how to deal with an incident and how to analyze breach of an Oracle database. GDPR will change how companies in all the parts of the world process personal data from EU citizens. In the United States, almost every state has data breach and protection laws that are similar to GDPR.

Not only knowing how to deal with an incident is important and it makes absolutely no sense to leave the database wide open and prepare to deal with an incident breach. Clearly one of the most important steps you can take *now* is to protect the database and try to prevent a potential breach. This is a very complex area and is discussed in more detail in a later section. If you can prevent most direct access to the database and ensure that every authorized user has the least privilege needed, as well as ensure that all of data has the best access controls possible, the only breach available is a corrupt employee with this limited correct access or an attacker who breaches an exploit in the application code.

Employing some level of Oracle security makes the most sense. Quite often sites have limited Oracle security even in this day and age. My experience of conducting security audits still causes me consternation and head scratching when I review customer databases and find them to be wide open. My discussion with the customer is on service availability and budget. There is often a push to get an application live in a database and no effort is expended on security during the design and build process. Quite often, applications are designed and built with privileged access with a lack of granularity or data access controls.

Still further, the DBA is often seen to be accessing the database with superuser privilege (sysdba) on a daily basis. This means there is very limited accountability, as it's often impossible to know who did what and when. Using highly privileged accounts also means that the staff can access any data they want to with impunity.

Designing practical and useful audit trails is beneficial to the results of future forensic analysis or investigations as well. Audit trails in the Oracle database using the standard features are also free. Designing practical audit trails is not free in the sense of the hours and effort required to design, implement, and maintain them, but using the standard features of the database means there are no license fees. If implemented correctly, an audit trail can be up and running very quickly; the section on designing audit trails illustrates this with the free toolkit written in PL/SQL and SQL. It can be implemented to get policy driven audit and alerts for your database.

Audit trails should be cheap compared to actual hardening, For example, if you identify that accounts of the database have weak passwords and no password management features are enabled, it would take quite a bit of effort to design controls. Designing password management should be simple but applications and other working practices often get in the way of having a password expire after 30, 60, or 90 days.

Enforcing complex passwords also causes problems for the people who have used the same password for the last 14 years and that password is five characters long. Obviously, it's easy to remember these without writing them down, but obviously many other people are likely to know it and have guessed it over the years. Implementing controls such as these can be complex, and implementing audits to understand who is connecting as a particular account or who is attempting to connect is simple in comparison.

The security of the database should initially include a detailed audit trail. This will help you understand what security issues have potentially been exploited or abused and it will certainly give you a detailed audit trail with any potential forensic analysis. Although audit trails are cheap and cheerful and will tell you what's happening, don't ignore securing and locking down the database. Security of the database costs money; this is unfortunate but a fact of life. It is better to be pragmatic and understand your budget in advance for security and then spend it very wisely. Always aim to get the best protection for the least amount of money spent. Often this starts with audit trails.

Having a detailed audit trail will ensure that evidence will always exist to use in any analysis.

Ensure that data security and auditing are part of your ongoing process; to reiterate, it makes no sense to plan for a potential attack that might not happen while not actually protecting the assets. Common sense!

Coming back to incident response and forensic analysis, ensure that the planning takes place, and ensure that an incident response process has been developed, reviewed, and agreed. Ensure that all relevant personnel who deal with an incident are fully aware of the contents of the plan and know what to do and how to act in case of a breach.

Ensure that you've built your team in advance and everyone who was part of the team knows what to do. Ensure that you have collected the relevant tools needed for the incident response. These tools should be available easily at the drop of a hat for the relevant staff to use when necessary.

Pre-test the tools ensure all relevant staff are familiar with them. Use them, understand what they do, and understand what the results look like. This will help with any future analysis. Using tools for the first time in an analysis situation is a mistake. If you use the tools on a clean database with no breach, you going to see normal day-to-day business and know what it looks like so that when a breach does occur, you know what non-standard actions also look like.

Assume an attack will happen, prepare the process and document, assign a leader, gather tools, build a team, and train it in advance.

Thinking About Database Security

It makes no sense to create a detailed process for dealing with a potential Oracle database breach or incident unless you also take steps to protect that same Oracle database from being attacked in the first place. This would be like sitting at your dining room table, pre-writing a letter to the police that describes how your house was burgled just in case it ever is, while at the same time removing the locks from all of your doors.

Performing security audits of an Oracle database, defining a security policy, and locking an Oracle database could be the subject of a complete book. This section covers these topics very briefly.

Securing an Oracle database can be a big and complex task; the biggest factor that determines the security level that you can achieve for your databases is budget or the money available to allocate to Oracle security.

Do not attempt to secure your Oracle databases in an ad hoc or random manner. An ad hoc technique will in the end provide very little security. I have seen many sites over the last 16 years of performing security audits of Oracle databases whereby the customer seems to have a random set of controls in combination with gaping holes.

The first step in securing an Oracle database is to understand what you have currently. The best way to do this is to perform a detailed security audit of at least one production database. Learn as much as possible about what is wrong with one valuable production database and use that information to develop a security policy to lock down and secure all of your Oracle databases.

There are a number of possibilities to perform a security audit of the Oracle database:

- **Hire someone**: This is probably the quickest and most cost-effective because you can hire someone with the relevant skill who can perform an audit very quickly and provide a detailed report. But longer term, this does not build up the skill in your own organization.

- **Use a commercial tool**: It is possible to purchase a license for a commercial Oracle security scanner and use this to perform a detailed audit of a single database. In some circumstances, this can be more cost-effective than hiring an external consultant and it has the benefit that some limited skill is transferred internally by using the tool. The downside is that using a tool means that you only get the output of the tool itself without any additional analysis and annotation from an expert. Figure 6-1 shows an example completed security scan of an Oracle database using the commercial tool called PFCLScan.

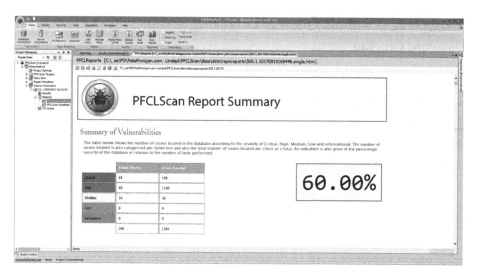

Figure 6-1. *An Oracle database vulnerability scan with PFCLScan of an Oracle 12.2 database*

- **Build your own tools or use free tools**: Constructing Oracle security tools internally is a good option. The knowledge gained in writing and using them is kept internally . Free tools can be downloaded and used conjunction with internal built tools. Listing 6-1 shows a sample password cracking session using a free PL/SQL password cracker at http://www.petefinnigan.com/oracle_password_cracker.htm. A reasonable amount of cost is involved in creating these tools, but there are no ongoing license fees.

The output of a detailed Oracle security audit, combined with existing security policies (including any detailed Oracle security policy if one exists) and any best practices, create a detailed Oracle security policy specific to the organization. The security policy should be a succinct as possible.

Listing 6-1. A Sample Password Cracking Session with A PL/SQL
Password Cracker

```
SQL> @cracker-v2.9.sql
PL/SQL cracker: Release 2.9.0.0.0 - Production on Tue Jun 06
01:15:59 2017
Copyright (c) 2008 - 2017 PeteFinnigan.com Limited. All rights
reserved.
```

T [Username	] [P(10g)]	[Password (11g)	] FL ST
U [SYS	] [	] [oracle1	] DI OP
U [AUDSYS	] [	] [AUDSYS	] PU EL
U [SYSTEM	] [	] [oracle1	] DI OP
U [SYSBACKUP	] [	] [D_SYSBKPW	] DE EL
U [SYSDG	] [	] [D_SYSDGPW	] DE EL
U [SYSKM	] [	] [D_SYSKMPW	] DE EL
U [SYSRAC	] [	] [D_SYSRACPW	] DE EL
U [OUTLN	] [	] [outln	] PU EL
U [XS$NULL	] [	] [	] -- EL
U [GSMADMIN_INTERNAL	] [	] [gsm	] DE EL
U [GSMUSER	] [	] [gsm	] DE EL
U [DIP	] [	] [dip	] PU EL
U [DBSFWUSER	] [	] [SECURE123	] DE EL
U [ORACLE_OCM	] [	] [OCM_3XP1R3D	] DE EL
U [SYS$UMF	] [	] [sysumf	] DE EL
U [DBSNMP	] [	] [dbsnmp	] PU EL
U [APPQOSSYS	] [	] [APPQOSSYS	] PU EL
U [GSMCATUSER	] [	] [gsm	] DE EL
U [GGSYS	] [	] [ggsys	] PU EL
U [XDB	] [	] [XDB	] PU EL
U [ANONYMOUS	] [IMP {}]	[	] IM EL

184

```
U [WMSYS                   ] [        ] [wmsys                  ] PU EL
U [OJVMSYS                 ] [        ] [xxx                    ] DE EL
U [CTXSYS                  ] [        ] [CTXSYS                 ] PU EL
U [ORDSYS                  ] [        ] [ordsys                 ] PU EL
U [ORDDATA                 ] [        ] [orddata                ] PU EL
U [ORDPLUGINS              ] [        ] [ordplugins             ] PU EL
U [SI_INFORMTN_SCHEMA      ] [        ] [si_informtn_schema     ] PU EL
U [MDSYS                   ] [        ] [mdsys                  ] PU EL
U [OLAPSYS                 ] [        ] [no_password            ] DE EL
U [MDDATA                  ] [        ] [MDDATA                 ] PU EL
U [SPATIAL_CSW_ADMIN_USR] [        ] [spatial_csw_admin_usr] PU EL
U [DVSYS                   ] [        ] [                       ] -- EL
U [LBACSYS                 ] [        ] [LabelSecurity12_#      ] DE EL
U [DVF                     ] [        ] [                       ] -- EL
U [HR                      ] [        ] [                       ] -- EL
U [PETE                    ] [        ] [pete                   ] PU OP
U [PETE2                   ] [        ] [pete2                  ] PU OP
U [PETE3                   ] [        ] [pete3                  ] PU OP
U [PETE4                   ] [        ] [pete4                  ] PU OP
U [PETE5                   ] [        ] [pete5                  ] PU OP
U [PETE6                   ] [PETE6 ] [pete6                  ] PU OP
```

INFO: Number of crack attempts = [68691]
INFO: Elapsed cracking time = [3.97 Seconds]
INFO: Total elapsed time = [3.98 Seconds]
INFO: Cracks per second = [17300]

PL/SQL procedure successfully completed.

SQL>

It is important that there is a budget to implement the policy in all relevant Oracle databases. It is also important that it is possible to implement every clause of the policy in all Oracle databases. The Oracle security policy should contain three broad areas of actions that make up its content:

- **Security patching (10%)**: Security patches should be applied on a consistent and regular basis. Oracle releases quarterly security patch set of dates (PSUs) and, without applying these, it is often impossible to be secure against exploits reported to Oracle.

- **Hardening (30%)**: Hardening is an important component of securing an Oracle database. Hardening removes access to data dictionary components and dangerous facilities. It also applies secure settings to various database parameters. Locking down will also generally enable things like password management and remove extraneous services and features.

- **Design work (60%)**: The security design work is the most complex. This will generally include data access controls and user security. It should also include context-based security, network controls, operating system controls, and much more. This involves the general security settings and work is needed to secure the application in the Oracle database from abuse.

These areas are broken into percentages to give a broad indication of the importance of each section of Oracle security work. Although patching seems the smallest, that does not diminish its importance. Patching is the smallest percentage because, from the security auditor's perspective, it's a simple yes/no question and answer—is the database patched or not. Patching a database can be a complex procedure involving downtime, regression testing, and much more. Hardening is the next largest area and will in general improve the security of a particular database, but it will not improve the security of the data itself in the database. Hardening usually speaks to a core empty database, not an actual application and its settings. The design element is the most complex and hardest to achieve because it is specific to each application.

What this means is that a security policy that includes the three elements can be implemented as a two-phased process. When a database is provisioned, it can be locked down and patched to the hardening standard. Once an application is deployed, then application within the database can be further locked down. Until the application is deployed, it's not possible to know the requirements of individual user accounts and schemas or the data access requirements.

Database security policy should be written that takes all of this into account. It should be possible that once a database has been built and deployed and an application installed, an automated security audit check should be possible to confirm that the database security policy has been fully implemented and that the database is compliant.

Enabling Sophisticated Audit Trails

The subject of designing practical and sophisticated audit trails for an Oracle database could fill a whole book. This section simply summarizes the high-level requirements of a suitable audit trail design.

The key message that comes from any Oracle incident response and forensic analysis is that it would have been so much easier if an audit trail had existed in the database that captured the actions of the attacker. It's impossible to go back and add audit trails for an attack that has already occurred, but quite clearly it makes great sense to take some time now to design and implement useful and sophisticated audit trails so that if there is an attack, an audit trail exists to make the analysis process much easier.

An audit trail design should not be ad hoc. It makes no sense to randomly add settings. An audit trail should be designed on the basis of "I want to know". You must start with a list of issues that you want to capture, such as:

- Anyone logging in or out

- Anyone masquerading as a DBA

- Attempted SQL Injections

- Changes to user profiles

- Changes to database structure

This design should be based on capturing actions in the database that should not be occurring. This should be specified without technical know-how. Specifications should be documented at a high-level design or policy perspective. This can be signed off on and agreed to in advance of implementation.

Only after the policy has been designed should the actual technical solution be specified. There are many types of audit solutions that can be used with Oracle. At a high level, these include the features that come for free with the database, the cost options such as audit vault, and any third-party solutions available from a multitude of vendors.

The solutions available inside the database include the core audit, unified audit, fine-grained audit, trigger-based audit, and many more. The design should also include all the other elements required for an audit solution. It should include storage specification and sizing, design of archiving and purge, performance considerations, management alerting and escalation, and much more.

A comprehensive audit solution should also include audits of the audit trail itself. If an attacker attempts to delete an audit record, that action will also be captured.

Figure 6-2 shows an audit trail solution written in approximately 14k lines of PL/SQL and SQL code. The origin of this toolkit came from working with clients over the last eight years, whereby they wanted sophisticated and useful audit trails in the database but did not have the budget, team size, or time to design something and implement it.

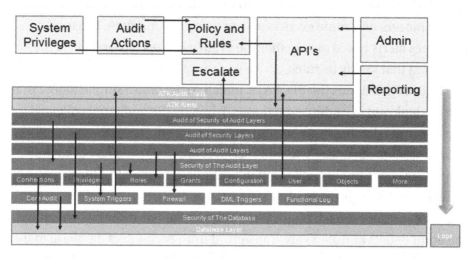

Figure 6-2. *PFCLATK, a design for a simple audit trail toolkit for Oracle (c) Copyright 2017 PeteFinnigan.com Limited. Used with Permission.*

This toolkit is called PFCLATK. The main idea behind it is to allow someone to simply install a single script into an Oracle database that enables sophisticated audit trail. The only things the user needs to do is to select which policies they want to enable and to potentially add some factors. The factors are things such as IP addresses of DBAs, the names of DBA users, the names of schemas, and so on. This meant that someone could literally spend no more than 5 to 10 minutes setting up and installing an audit trail. The toolkit is very sophisticated and includes many layers. Not only can you enable built-in policies, there are also policies that include audits of audits—audit security and audit security audit. These layers enable you to capture anyone attempting to change the audit trails.

The toolkit is policy based, but these policies are not the same as the unified audit in Oracle 12c. The policies combine the collection of raw audit trail details and events. The audit policy can collect data from multiple sources, including core audit, trigger-based audit, function-based audit, and others. The alerts process the collected audit data based on the specified time cycle. Some events can be immediate, some events can run once a month, and some events can run every few minutes. The toolkit generates alerts based on whether the event captures any actions in the audit trail that satisfy its rules.

Figure 6-3 extends the PFCLATK toolkit to become a simple toolkit that can be deployed to multiple databases, whereby the audit trail collected in each target database can be automatically transferred back to a single central storage database. The same script is applied to a target as to the central storage. Simple configuration is required to specify if the target is the central storage or simply a target. Once deployed a simple setup is required to connect each target to the central storage. After this is enabled, the audit details and alerts are transferred from each target database to the central storage every hour. This means that the storage required for this audit toolkit in each target database is limited, because every hour the data is extracted and purged. This is cost-effective in terms of storage.

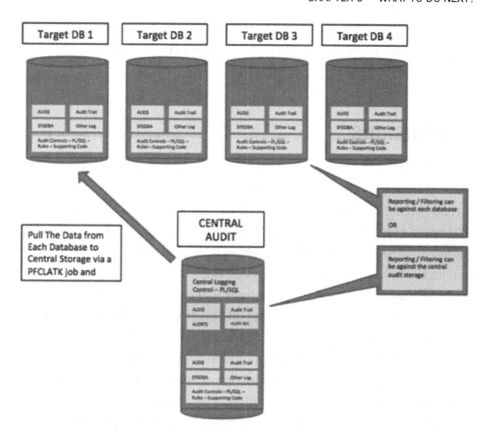

Figure 6-3. *PFCLATC, a design for a simple audit trail toolkit for Oracle (c) Copyright 2017 PeteFinnigan.com Limited. Used with Permission.*

The main purpose of this toolkit is to enable customers to download simple set of scripts, make some very simple configuration changes, and then deploy to each target database and set up a centralized storage database for audit trails of all databases. This means that reporting can also be centralized for all databases by targeting a single database. The toolkit is free and is available by e-mailing pete@petefinnigan.com. The toolkit is just an API and does not include any reporting, but it does have one or two simple reports related to the extract and archive processes. Some simple management screens and reports will be added to PFCLScan to enable customers to use the free toolkit. It also includes an easy-to-use graphical user interface. That said, you are free to use the command-line toolkit if you want; just contact me to ask for a download.

Conclusions

I hope you enjoyed this journey through Oracle incident response and forensic analysis. I hope you've learned what to do if your own systems are perhaps breached. Even though Oracle forensics has been around since 2004 when I first wrote about it in the Sans 509 class, there's been no major public progress in terms of free or commercial tools that would help deal with an incident. That said, it is perfectly viable to analyze a database for a potential breach using the standard tools that come with a database.

One of the key tenets of analyzing an Oracle database for a potential breach is to plan for it. This is very important to ensure that anything you do does not destroy or change any potential evidence that could be used later. Factor in large databases, production scenarios where it is simply not as easy as analyzing a PC, and different techniques need to be used. With a PC you can simply copy the disk and analyze the copy to produce evidence. With a 200TB database that needs to be up 99.99% of the time, this is not realistic. Most sites would not have enough disk space or time to copy all of the database anyway.

It's also very important that you plan exactly what you're going to do in terms of steps, analysis, and tools to use. Make sure that a team is set up to handle an incident; ideally people are selected from a different channel in the business. In this way, this person can manage the process and ensure all steps are taken, and it's less likely that he would change or miss steps because of the need to cover things up.

Understanding that the incident has occurred is hard; this is primarily because there are so many different types of possible incidents that can occur with an Oracle database and it's very difficult to plan and identify all these. Combine this with a myriad of possibilities in terms of data location and data access and we are left with two common scenarios.

The first is that data has been stolen and located somewhere else (such as on Twitter). The second is that some change has occurred to the database that no one can explain. Taking these two tenets as a starting point is a reasonable strategy. Once the incident has been understood to have occurred, the incident response process must be activated. The primary purpose of this process is to establish the true incident has occurred, collect as much forensic evidence as possible before it could possibly be changed, make decisions on what to do the database in terms of getting the business back working, and finally make a forensic analysis.

Forensic analysis is complex and cannot really be identified in advance, again for the same reasons that there are so many different possibilities, it's very difficult to do this. Key things should be achieved. The first is to establish the start and end time and date of the potential attack and then collect evidence between these two timestamps from all possible systems and locations. This evidence can be filtered and organized in a time-ordered format so that the attacker's actions can be extracted from common day-to-day business actions. The case can then be built against the attacker to prove exactly what he did, how he gained access, what data he saw, and finally what could he have done if he had more skill.

In advance of any potential incident, it is clearly very important that database security is considered. If an incident can be prevented by having good database security, it is worth doing. Having a comprehensive and sophisticated audit trail will go a long way toward this goal. In parallel, all the elements for incident response should be prepared in advance to ensure that if an incident does occur, you're able and skilled to deal with it.

Further Reading

Despite Oracle forensics first being talked and written about more than 13 years ago, there is been very little published in recent times. I have presented Oracle forensics topics at various conferences over the years and as recently as 2017. Here is a short list of some useful papers, links, and web sites to find out more about Oracle forensics. The list is not exhaustive. Bear in mind a lot of these are quite old at the time of writing of this book, but may still be useful.

- Pete Finnigan (2003). *Detecting SQL Injection in Oracle.* http://www.securityfocus.com/infocus/1714. Some forensics ideas, such as mining redo, SQL extraction, trace, and audit.

- Pete Finnigan (2004). *Oracle Forensics Module 17.* Original SANS 509 6-Day Oracle security training.

- Arup nanda (2005). Mining for clues at http://www.oracle.com/technology/oramag/oracle/05-jul/o45dba.html.

- Alex Gorbachev (2006). Log Miner for forensics. http://www.pythian.com/blogs/269/oracle-logminer-helps-investigate-security-issues.

- Paul Wright (2006/7). A number of papers at http://www.oracleforensics.com and his SANS GSOC paper http://www.sans.org/reading_room/whitepapers/application/ for the final exam after attending the SANS Oracle 509 class.

- Pete Finnigan (2007). Oracle Forensics. http://www.petefinnigan.com/Oracle_Forensics.pdf. Presented at UKOUG conference 2007 and multiple other venues.

- David Litchfield (2007). Six-part paper. `http://www.databasesecurity.com/`.

- Alejandro Vargas (2007). Log Miner 10g Implementation Example. `http://static7.userland.com/oracle/gems/alejandroVargas/logminerexample.pdf`.

- David Litchfield (2007). Blackhat paper. `http://www.databasesecurity.com/dbsec/forensics.ppt`.

- Two books (Note: one of the books is not available):

    - *Oracle Forensics* by Paul Wright (2007. ISBN-10-0977671526.

    - Oracle Forensics Analysis Using the Forensic Examiners Database Scalpel (FEDS) Tool (2008). ISBN-10: 047019118X *Never written or released??*

- Pete Finnigan (2007). Oracle Incident response and forensics. Presented at Technology SIG UKOUG, Manchester. Not published.

Index

© Pete Finnigan 2018
P. Finnigan, *Oracle Incident Response and Forensics*,
https://doi.org/10.1007/978-1-4842-3264-4

Get the eBook for only $5!

Why limit yourself?

With most of our titles available in both PDF and ePUB format, you can access your content wherever and however you wish—on your PC, phone, tablet, or reader.

Since you've purchased this print book, we are happy to offer you the eBook for just $5.

To learn more, go to http://www.apress.com/companion or contact support@apress.com.

Apress®

Printed in the United States
By Bookmasters